The Sergeant Major's Wife

A Reflection

Billie-Fae Gerard Gill

ISBN: 1548500585
ISBN 13: 9781548500580

FOR MY GRANDPARENTS

Fabian and Anna (Nyquist) Anderson
Harley and Hattie-Becky (Dye) Leonard

What is an Army Wife?
Author Unknown

AN ARMY WIFE is mostly girl. But there are times, such as when her husband is away and she is mowing the lawn or fixing a flat tire on a youngster's bike that she begins to suspect she is also boy. She usually comes in three sizes: petite, plump and pregnant. During the early years of her marriage it is often hard to determine which size is her normal size.

She has babies all over the world and measures time in terms of places as other women do in years. "It was at Leavenworth that we all had the mumps...in Tokyo, Dad was promoted. At least one of her babies was born or a transfer was accomplished while she was alone. This causes her to suspect a secret pact between her husband and the Army providing for a man to be overseas or on temporary duty at times such as those.

An army wife is international. She may be an Iowa farm girl, a French Mademoiselle, Japanese doll or an ex-Army nurse. When discussing Army problems, they all speak the same language. She can be a great actress. To heart-broken children at transfer time she gives an Academy Award performance. "Arizona is going to be such fun! I hear they have Indian reservations, and tarantulas, and rattlesnakes!" But her heart is breaking with theirs. She wonders if this Army is worth the sacrifices.

An ideal Army wife has the patience of an angel, the flexibility of putty, the wisdom of a scholar and the stamina of a horse. If she dislikes money it helps. She is sentimental carrying her memories with her in an old footlocker. She is a dreamer when she vows" "We'll never move again!" An optimist: "The next place will be better." A realist: "Oh, well as long as we are together."

One might say she's a bigamist sharing her husband with a demanding entity called duty. When duty calls, she becomes No. 2 wife. Until she accepts this fact, her life can be miserable. She is, above all, a woman who married a soldier who offered her the permanency of a gypsy, the miseries of loneliness, the frustration of conformity and the security of love. Sitting among her packing boxes with squabbling children nearby, she is sometimes willing to chuck it all…. until she hears the firm step and the cheerful voice of that lug who gave her all this. Then she is happy to be…his Army wife.

The Author At Age 20

Author's Notes

I EXPERIENCED SLEEPLESS nights and shed tears writing *The Sergeant Major's Wife* because as I wrote I was forced to relive both good and bad experiences in order to paint the picture of my life with an unvarnished brush. Editorial selection excluded some important players on the stage of my life, and although you do not appear, you are cherished. Thank you, Alveda Rhude, John Shaw, Dorothy Gill, Tamara Shoulders, Cesario Ferrar Ferrar, and scores of events—Mark's swearing in as a naturalized citizen in Columbia, South Carolina—and others. I also thank my husband, Bill, prior military sons who read the earliest manuscript and gave approval, and other members of my family who helped in various ways—I couldn't have done it without you. And a special bear hug and warmest thanks to new friends N. K. (an Army wife,) and Bonnie, both younger members of MAC, a writers' group who kept me writing and helped get it published by trying to teach computer skills to me. (Impossible) And, thank you, Cousin Dan, my tech support guy—you were always there for me as was Tom Hyman, well-known best-selling author, professional editor, teacher and friend. Special thanks to Carole, one of the first people I met in North Carolina, for your dream about going on a book tour together and for your sharp eye proofing. Thanks also to readers Donna and Denise, and long, long-time friends Pati and Marion—any pain I have felt as a result of turning myself inside out becomes worthwhile if you enjoyed reading this book. There are others who helped, you know who you are—thank you for sharing your computer skills, spelling and friendship. You are all amazing.

Why did I write this story? N.K. Wagner pointed out that I lived at the right time in all the wrong places, and Bonnie said, "Wow! I didn't know about *that*!" Together they convinced me to share my unique story by presenting the human side of historical events (1949-1969) and by demonstrating the role of the distaff side of Army life to show readers what it's really like—not Hollywood's version—to be a military family.

The Sergeant Major's Wife turns a spotlight on the military occupation of West Germany following World War II, the 1950 invasion of South Korea, the Cold War, the Cuban missile crisis, the defoliation mistake in Southeast Asia, and exposes little known secrets of Army life. William Thomas Gill, Regular Army, Retired, MOS-00Z50—my husband, said combat veterans rarely discuss their life or death experiences. For that reason Bill's highly decorated military career is left for some other writer to discern from official records. The Sergeant Major's Wife is my story, not his.

Grandfather Fabian Anderson, a proud naturalized Swedish-American, was opposed to involuntary conscription but that didn't stop his fourteen-year-old American born son, Emmett, from enlisting in the Army in 1917. A paternal great-uncle served in France in *"the war to end wars"* and later suffered from shellshock. My maternal grandmother spoke often of her father's role as "defender of our nation's honor" meaning his 1861-1865 enlistment in the Union Army and proudly extolled her grandfather's role in the Continental Army, or praised her son-in-law, Uncle George, for his overseas service in World War I.

None of that information provided a clue about how to be an Army wife. Since I didn't drown in the choppy sea of matrimony and our marriage lasted sixty-one years perhaps it was—as Bill believed--preordained.

A little poetic license moved the story along, I changed a couple of names and created conversations from facts—when actual words couldn't be known. Names of actual persons living or dead and real places or events described are accurate to the best of my ability. Revised. March 2018. All errors are mine.

With special gratitude to my two anonymous admirers and one very special librarian. Thank you.

Billie-Fae Gerard Gill
Danbury Forest, North Carolina 28625
© 3 July 2013

Preface

WE WERE A tightly knit family of three. Mother was an unemployed, college educated gym teacher and Daddy a music teacher and concert violinist. They lost our house, car and nearly everything else during The Great Depression of 1929. When I was four we lived rent free in a lovely brick house belonging to Daddy's friend who was on tour in Europe. For a while that summer we also lived in a tent pitched on the shore of Lake Chautauqua near Bemus Point. One night it poured so hard the tent collapsed and we had to go to my grandparents' already crowded house a few days until Daddy found us a place to live.

Ultimately evicted from a cold-water flat in downtown Jamestown, but before suffering the indignity of actually being thrown out on the street, Daddy decided it was time for us to move to a larger city where there might be a job opportunity. It was difficult in western New York State to find work and millions of good people remained unemployed the spring of 1941.

We left our Swedish relatives in Jamestown and relocated to Erie County in northwestern Pennsylvania sixty miles away. Daddy was hopeful his chances for a job—any job—might improve. By then he was willing to put aside a music career he had studied for longer than fifteen years for a job with a steady paycheck.

We were lucky! The General Electric hired him to read blue prints. We bought a four bedroom brick house in suburban Lawrence Park, filled the pantry, and breathed a sigh of relief.

I knew toys were made in Japan, but until kamikaze pilots shocked the world at Pearl Harbor that's about all I knew. December eighth President Roosevelt announced we were at war, the draft board classified Daddy an essential war worker, Mother became an Air Raid Warden, and I was given the ongoing task of being the new kid in second grade at Priestley Avenue Grade School.

During the war years (1941-1945) General Electric manu-factured M-I rifle parts instead of refrigerators, we bought black-out shades, and Daddy worked third shift. We bought war bonds and saving stamps, collected grease and tin cans, got used to cars, shoes, meat, sugar, gas, and other items being rationed. We tasted, and hated, ugly white oleomargarine—a substitute for butter and tried to drink Postum. Daddy was earning a good salary; we had money now, but there was little we could buy.

Our school teachers warned us to stay out of Lake Erie because it was rumored the enemy might try to poison the water, and every school day we rehearsed hiding in case of enemy attack. Some changes are good, but others hurt. By the time I was grown up you couldn't see the scars from those early years, but they were there. They were buried deep.

In June of 1951 I had earned a high school diploma and a four year academic scholarship to a local college for women. I was an attractive, popular girl at a loss about what to do with the rest of her life. When I asked my parents they said it was up to me to trim my sails and wait for a tailwind. I thought about *Pitcairn Island, The Sea Wolf* and other books about the sea and doubted I would know how to sail my own ship.

Mother said, "When it's time you'll know what to do."

Daddy said I could live with them as long as I wished but I saw Mother shaking her head and knew it would never work.

"Every mouse needs its own hole, honey. You'll do great," she said. "When it's time to seek your fortune, you'll know."

I tried parttime jobs as a secretary in a music store, waitressing in a busy diner, and day camp counselor at the Erie YWCA on Presque Isle at Lake Erie. For months I floundered. Should I go to college, complete the nursing program I'd begun at Hamot Hospital, or settle for a job in a manufacturing plant —probably the local GE—like many of my classmates? There was one other possibility for girls like me. I could get married. I rejected that option as improbable. I was too young to even think about marriage.

By the spring of 1952 I had exhausted all but one of those options and worked in the typing pool of the Billing Department in a large factory. It was monotonous and I hated it. My spirits soared when I learned of a pending general layoff. I found my supervisor, Dorrie, in her office and begged to be in the first echelon. She expressed shock.

"No! You're one of our best typists!" she exclaimed. I couldn't hide my disappointment. "Well, if that's how you feel, then quit," she said. So, I did.

Filled with relief, but still unsure about my future, I hurried home to cogitate. I had some important decisions to make and it was time for me to check the gib boom, get out of dry dock, and make up my mind which way to sail.

A boy I had been dating—fairly steadily—signed on as a merchant mariner which kept him out of the state for months at a time. I considered alternatives. Waiting for him wasn't one.

I didn't like the color of the uniform for WACs, but the Navy uniform was very trim, a nice shade of blue, and would look good on me. I told Daddy I might join the United States Navy. Fists flailing and red faced he roared, "Over my dead body!"

When the dog barked I went out to meet the mailman who handed me a small envelope that turned out to be an invitation from Nancy, an old school friend, who lived now with her parents in Arlington, Virginia. Nirvana! I wouldn't have to vegetate in my parents' house. I could put to sail with a port in sight. I phoned to accept and learned her father worked at National Archives and could help me get a job.

In the background a WLEU news announcer prattled on about possible peace in some place called "Kor-e-ah." Wherever that place was, it had nothing to do with me. I'd had enough war talk to last a lifetime. I turned off the radio and looked out the window.

The afternoon sky was pinkish-red with no signs of a squall; it was time for me to get out of the doldrums—I had no idea how to accomplish that—but it was time.

I didn't own a sea bag so I tossed all I owned into a small brown suitcase. Armed with hutzpah and ten dollars I told Mother and Daddy good-bye, climbed aboard the midnight Greyhound head-ed to Washington, D.C., and left home without a clue about what waited for me there.

CHAPTER 1

— ✼ —

The Fast Talker

WHEN NANCY MET me at the bus station I was unprepared to hear what she said. I was hot, dusty, tired from the long bus ride, and looked forward to going to bed early.

"You're not serious, are you? Can't you phone and say I'm too tired, or something? I really don't go on blind dates. Not ever. Especially, not after I've ridden eighteen hours on a grungy, smoke filled, uncomfortable bus!"

Nancy was a determined matchmaker and insisted Bill and I were *"perfect for each other."* I remained very reluctant and a little leery about dating a soldier, but because I was her house guest I felt obligated and allowed Nancy to coax me into agreeing.

"Okay," I said, "but you and that friend of Bill's you mentioned… Cliff something or other? Bill's roommate? You two have to double date with us, or I'm not going."

I didn't wait long before Bill and Cliff arrived sporting twin GI haircuts and reeking of Old Spice. They swaggered into the living room and stood there trying to convince Nancy to put in a good word with her friend, Bobbie, a USO dancer Cliff wanted to date.

"I know it's against USO rules, but you can convince her, can't you?" Cliff said. "Do that and Bill will be happy to escort your visitor"—that being me—"this evening."

Then Bill saw me, smiled, and asked what I would like to do. I had never been to Washington before and suggested visiting Lincoln Memorial or touring Washington.

"No, ma'am," Bill drawled. "Let's go ride that big 'ole roller coaster I heard tell about. Okay, Cliff? Nancy?"

Egad! We are polar opposites! I enjoyed movies, concerts, opera, ballet— apparently foreign choices for Bill who also discarded my suggestion to go dancing. I found myself wondering why I was climbing into the back seat of his fancy new Buick with Nancy in front beside Cliff who was driving.

Bill said he'd recently returned from the war in Korea. I told him I was getting a job in D.C. and had a boyfriend in the merchant navy sailing somewhere on The Great Lakes. He claimed he had a girlfriend "back home in Carolina." This was followed by a surprising confession.

"I never have gone on a blind date before and had to be bribed into this one. Cliff owes me big time. But now that we've met I'm glad I came. Don't worry," he said, "I'll be good and treat you like you were my little sister."

"Really?" My WOLF ALERT alarm screamed danger, look out! I'd been dating four years and thought: *uh huh. For Nancy I'll endure one date, but no more. Apparently, this guy thinks I am an idiot.* I had heard lines like that before. I began to count the minutes until it would be time to go home and dump this jerk who acted like he thought he was God's gift to women! "Do you even *have* a little sister?"

The braggart shrugged and said he sorta did have and her name was Sonja.

I began answering questions monosyllabically. In spite of such cool behavior I suspected he'd want a second date. What should I do? I didn't want to be mean or rude about it. I decided to brush him off politely, but firmly. After all, it was just one blind date and

2

he'd be out of my life forever. Things didn't pan out quite the way I anticipated. Before we returned to Nancy's house he did ask if I'd go on a single date the next day. It shocked us both when without hesitation, I agreed.

Once he made up his mind about anything it was *Katie bar the door* and don't get in the way. Making a marriage proposal on our first date was typical behavior. And it was no surprise—except to me, when he declared I *would* marry him. In fact, if it hadn't been against Army Regulations he might have dragged me into his cave as soon as we met.

Bill was the kind of man who seized the moment, flew by the seat of his pants, and never took no for an answer. He began to woo me with candy, flowers, movies, and sweet talk. But he was moving way too fast. I realized Bill was no high school boy; I was in over my head if I couldn't quickly think of a way to politely turn down his marriage proposals and cool him off.

"If I agree to marry you will you go and leave me in peace?" He promised; he lied.

Others had asked me to marry them but none so persistently. Since my ruse didn't work I tried something else. Something I'd never done before, I told an audacious lowdown, dirty rotten fib. Actually, it was a big, fat lie.

"I have something to confess," I began, casting my eyes down for effect, "I have negro blood. Understand? Part colored, high yellow? Mulatto? Sorry. I can't marry you. "

In the 1950s nice well brought up white gentlemen—especially men like Bill—who were reared south of the Mason/Dixon Line, might have a colored girlfriend but would never consider marrying interracially. When I lied with a straight face and said I was mulatto it should've stopped him. Permanently.

After pausing a nanosecond he said, "I don't care what color you are. Marry me."

In a last ditch attempt I said, "I have a girlfriend, Pati. She's smart, nice, beautiful and currently unattached. I can introduce you."

He said he didn't need to meet anyone else. I could fight, flee or give up. I didn't want to kill him or go back home to suburban Erie, Pennsylvania. I was out of alibis, exhausted, and knew he would not quit proposing until I accepted. Raising an imaginary white flag I surrendered, like Lee did to Grant.

"Okay. You win. We're engaged." It was June of 1952. I was still eighteen.

The following day Bill paid an Alexandria jewelry store a month's wages for a diamond ring. When friends in North Carolina and Pennsylvania heard about it they were aghast and predicted disaster. They begged us to realize love at first sight is a myth. They tried to dissuade us by pointing out I'd been out of high school less than two years, we had just met, it was a crazy idea, and I was too young to get married.

CHAPTER 2

— ✁ —

Carolina Shuffle

IT WAS TRUE that I was still a teen and I don't recommend brief court-ships or teenage brides, but in spite of all the reasonable objections and hurdles we were wed that July third in the chapel at Fort Belvoir, Virginia.

Both of us were more-or-less accustomed to getting our own way. It was obvious that two chiefs in one tepee might result in a fight to the finish, or require some fancy foot work. We decided not to fight. However, I wasn't good at ballroom dancing and needed a lot of practice. Blame it on my very early years as a ballerina en pointe.

Living together wasn't easy. Compromises littered the future of the charming, popular, football player turned career soldier, and the free thinking, risk taking, diminutive Yankee who accompanied him on his military journey and bore his seven children.

Like Elvis, another polite southern boy best known for singing, Bill preferred the Carolina Shuffle, a locally popular slow dance that kept partners folded in each other's arms while they swayed to soft romantic music. Frequently, for us, it was a whirling dervish, at other times a Viennese waltz, the Highland Fling, or Jitterbug. When I followed his lead James Cagney, Fred Astaire, and other famous dancers would have envied our ability to adapt to our crazy, crazy lifestyle because of the Carolina Shuffle.

Contrary to popular belief the wife of the sergeant major doesn't have an easy time. Sheer stubbornness—and the help we got from the Carolina Shuffle— kept us together when times were difficult, which was almost all of the time. There were multiple misunderstandings, real problems resulting from military orders, and little things worked out. For many years Bill thought he made all the decisions. But sometimes—both of us being very independent and stubborn—we had no choice. We had to agree to disagree.

I come from adventurous Welshmen and Vikings. Bill inherited a fighting spirit from his Scot-Irish ancestors. Neither of us was the type easily defeated, but we were realistic. Perhaps we never considered giving up because we knew how to make do, or do without, and we agreed hard work leads to success. More importantly, we maintained a strong faith in God which helped us face moves, children to care for, separations, illness, death, lack of money, and all the things other families experience.

First and foremost he was a soldier. Every time we parted we knew it might be for the last time and I knew that every time he went to work he might not return. With these circumstances, what held us together so long? Of course there were those kisses and though they helped it was a lot of prayers and a generous sprinkling of humor that helped us adapt to change and gave us the longevity spanning six decades.

Being able to adapt to change, and I had learned how to do that thanks to The Depression and The War, helps ensure a long marriage, but when people from differing backgrounds tempt fate by adding the variants of military life and a large family it takes adaptability, determination and discipline if you want to continue dancing with the same partner, and we did. And it takes the Carolina Shuffle.

Call me a dancing fool but I wasn't going to hoist the surrender flag, marry him, and then quit. To my way of thinking being a quitter is almost as bad as being a fink. We made a vow in church. I was in for the long haul and believed he was also. With that vision, and because we were lucky and blessed, we danced our way into the unknown.

To help us get started we took a cue from Lawrence Welk, the band leader who said, "and a one, and a two, and a three." If you nibble at problems with Welk's one, and two, and three approach big problems grow small, everything seems possible, and change becomes a friend.

I was on an intimate footing with change and had been most of my life. Change was still my constant companion the day I met Bill eleven years after the horrific Japanese attack on Honolulu. The Depression changed me, the war years had changed me, finishing high school and working in the factory changed me. I thought I knew all about change, but I had no idea of the myriad changes I would face as an Army wife or how often I would ask myself: Is that all there is?

CHAPTER 3

———— ✂ ————

Rules and Regulations

BETWEEN MEMORIAL DAY 1952 and The Fourth of July, I moved to Virginia, accepted a GS-5 clerical position in The Transportation Division of The Mutual Security Administration (Marshall Plan) in uptown D.C. at "K" and 17th Streets, and married Bill.

The capital city was overrun with uniformed men from every branch of the military. They were friendly and wanted to talk with me but I couldn't understand most of what they said because they used so many acronyms and code words. Army talk was another language I didn't speak like Swedish, Spanish, or German. I learned that A meant Able, B stood for Baker and C was Charlie. Once, when we were very young, I asked if C could stand for civilian instead of Charlie but Bill laughed and shook his head.

"We don't need a letter for civilians. Civilians? That's people like you, Babe."

Bill was bilingual—he spoke Southern and Army—using strange words and phrases I didn't know existed. It would take years for me to understand military lingo and just as long to learn unfamiliar idioms used by people in North Carolina. That meant I struggled to master two new languages until I became fluent enough to think the three Rs meant rank, rules and regulations instead of reading, 'riting and 'rithmetic, Z didn't stand for zebra but Zulu— a job description for a command sergeant major—going up street meant the same as going to town, and girls might say earbobs, not earrings.

Bill was a recently returned veteran of hand-to-hand fighting in Southeast Asia, and a decorated hero. I didn't know anything about the military pecking order, was ignorant about uniform insignias, ribbons, rules or regulations, and could barely recognize the difference between officers and enlisted soldiers. I questioned Bill about the uniforms.

He said M-44 was his winter "dress uniform" because it wasn't a work uniform. That made sense. Sorta. Then I asked why he called the jacket "Ike." He said World War II hero General Dwight D. "Ike" Eisenhower started it when he had one tailored for himself, minus stripes, of course.

In summer Bill wore a tan uniform with six yellow stripes, (three up and three rockers) on his sleeves to indicate his rank was E-7 master sergeant, whatever that was. He called the rows of multi-colored ribbons on his chest "salad" which made no sense, but he seemed proud of his salad. I understood it represented places he'd served and things he had done—like badges I could earn in the Girl Scouts, but his were for dramatically different things from mine.

"I got promoted real young. I've been told I'm the youngest master sergeant in the whole Army. Maybe it's true, Babe. I was promoted at twenty-one; who knows?"

All I said was, "Wow!" Naturally, I was familiar with the words master and sergeant, but never used together like that, and I had no idea what age a person should be to gain the rank of E-7, or even what an E-7 was. I was more interested in learning about other things. One day I asked if soldiers had summer and winter uniforms.

"Where I came from Labor Day is the time everyone religiously puts away white shoes, pocket books, hats, and all summer outfits until spring. Does the Army do that?"

"I'm required to wear Class A's—the M-44-- if I'm coming into town after mid- September. In the clinic we wear starched white uniforms. In Korea I wore different stuff. Combat stuff. Let's not talk any more about me. You look beautiful. Let's talk about your dress."

"It's blue. It's called a sheath and it's new." I said I preferred talking about him.   "Tell me how you, a medic, became the youngest master sergeant in the whole Army."

"Combat. People kept getting killed and I guess I was the only one qualified to get promoted so I got the rank. I went over there an E-1 litter bearer and returned an E-7 company clerk 'cause Herb, one of my school teachers, taught me to type. That's all."

Bill sounded modest and embarrassed. I doubted the Army promoted him just because he could type. Not knowing what to say I changed the subject again.

"Thanks for letting me drive your car, Bill. I put gas in the tank for you."

Bill tortured himself by imagining scenarios where on my way from Arlington to uptown D.C. other men made passes or accosted me on the bus on my way to work at Mutual Security Administration. He insisted on loaning his car to me with the stipulation that I would drive it to work and then to Fort Belvoir so we could go out before I had to return to Nancy's house in Arlington each night.

Bill didn't ask if I had a drivers' license. The first time I drove his car I realized a pattern of trust had been established and he expected me to return. After that I kept his car most nights and drove to meet him after work.

One evening I arrived a little late and dusk had begun shadowing the roads on Fort Belvoir. I hate being late. As soon as I drove on post I tried making up for lost time but a large group of marching soldiers with rifles and backpacks were in the middle of the road blocking my way. Why? Why do they have to be in the road? I was impatient and anxious to find Bill. I hit the horn. Beep, beep, beep. They ignored me. B-e-e-p! I had to slowly follow behind them. I told Bill about my frustrating experience.

"You beeped! At the cadre?" he gritted his teeth and continued, "Troops ALWAYS have the right of way!"

Oops! He seemed upset and concerned that he would be in trouble for what I'd done. The civilian me, capital Cee, wondered why they didn't restrict marching to the parade field, but I didn't ask. I apologized, but I still thought I was right and they were wrong.

"Sorry. Don't worry. You won't be in trouble. They saw it was me."

"You were driving my car? With my bumper sticker? They know whose car it was!"

I hadn't known military personnel are one hundred percent responsible for the actions of their guests and family members. That idea is taken seriously. The Army believes if a soldier can't maintain discipline and make people follow rules he is not a leader, and if not a leader, he is not promotable. I had innocently broken an important protocol, or some regulation, and done something against rules. I couldn't be punished for the infraction of beeping the horn at the marchers, but Bill might be.

"Oh. Sorry. I thought they were pedestrians who shouldn't be in the road."

I still thought I was right but didn't say any more and in a few minutes Bill acted like he had forgotten the incident.

About 8:00 PM, or twenty hundred hours, on a different hot, humid night we went swimming in the outdoor pool at Belvoir— I'd begun to say it that way like everyone else. Nobody said Fort, just Belvoir. Anyway, we were hot and tired and a swim seemed a good idea. I pointed out a NO SWIMMING AFTER DARK sign. Bill said to disregard it. I was dubious until bright headlight beams illuminated us. As soon as I read Militaary Police written in bold on the side of a jeep I no longer doubted. I knew. It was a catastrophe.

The FBI had just completed my background security clearance for MSA. Now it looked like I was going to be arrested by military police. If that happened my job was history, I was disgraced,and I would be back in Erie jobless.

"Anybody in that swimming pool?" a voice thick with authority demanded. I hid behind Bill.

"Nobody's in this pool." I was scared;Bill wasn't.

"Well, there better not be anybody swimming in there when I return either!"

I was shocked. Bill had lied to the military police and laughed. Needless to say, I wasn't laughing. I climbed out and he followed me trying to steal another kiss.

"I'm no law breaker, Will-i-am! I'm leaving. Right now!"

That night we cooled off in an air conditioned theater and afterwards shared chocolate milkshakes at The Hot Shoppe in nearby Alexandria.

A couple nights later we were parked at Hanes Point watching airplanes land at Andrews Air Force Base across the Potomac River when he proposed again. After I said yes he asked me to open the glove compartment. When I did it revealed a small velvet box. I guessed what it held—a sparkling solitaire diamond and white gold engagement ring that I slid onto my finger and heard him ask if we could get married right away.

"No. But we can get married in my church in Pennsylvania during Christmas vacation," I said, envisioning a beautiful winter wonderland ceremony in the Lutheran church.

A week later we decided we'd get married in September on my birthday. Why not? We were both employed adults. I'd been out of high school more than a year and Bill had already returned from war.

I said, "What are we waiting for? We know we're going to do it. Let's call our parents and tell them the wedding's next month in the chapel at Belvoir."

Bill contacted the chaplain who agreed to officiate at the ceremony. The next step was more difficult. In order to get a license we had to have my father's written and notarized permission because I still maintained residency in the Commonwealth of Pennsylvania where the age of majority was twenty-one. I phoned Mother and asked her to coerce Daddy into sending permission by reminding him I could get married in some state where his consent wasn't needed. We thought it was up to us to decide when to get married. We believed that, but first we had to jump through a number of hoops and some made me reconsider getting married to a soldier, in the chapel at Fort Belvoir, or even at all. Next we went to Fairfax County Court House where a bored female clerk advised us I needed a Wasserman blood test before a license could be issued. My hackles went up.

"Does he need to be tested for syphilis, too?" She shook her head. *How quaint! It's 1952! This is unfair!* "Why do I need a Wasserman, but not him? Why just me?"

"Army says so, and the State of Virginia. If you want to get married here *you* have to be tested for syphilis. No test, no license. I don't have all day. Make up your mind."

The next day I called a doctor near my office and was given an appointment during my lunch hour. The doctor failed four times to draw blood. After he tried behind my knee I fainted off the chair onto the floor and woke up on a lumpy leather couch in the waiting room. "No charge," the doctor said. "Go get married where blood testing isn't required."

Back at my desk I phoned Bill and explained what happened.

"We can't get a marriage license in Virginia," I said.

He had the car that day and said he'd pick me up after work and we'd go straight to the clinic at Belvoir. He was certain a corpsman could get the needed blood sample. Time dragged until five o'clock.

At Belvoir Bill explained our dilemma to a young man in a white uniform. A minute later that corpsman had wrapped a red rubber thingee around my arm and we all watched a little vial obediently fill. I learned two things: the Army takes care of its own, and let an experienced, well-trained, professional do the job.

We were set to get married. My father would be present to give me away. I had a new waltz length white dress and a white pillbox hat with a short white veil. Bill borrowed civvies, meaning not an Army uniform, and we placed a deposit on an apartment in Arlington. Everything was all arranged. Or, so I believed.

CHAPTER 4

— ✿ —

I Thee Wed, Maybe

BILL HAD EARNED a bronze star for valor under enemy fire in Korea but when it came to informing me of the hurdle lurking in the shadows of our wedding plans he was a lily-livered coward and afraid I wouldn't like it. He was certainly correct to think that. I didn't like it and that is an understatement.

"What!" I blurted out when he finally confessed. "Why do we have to ask your CO for permission? That is ludicrous. I don't even know his name. What business is it of his? You're well over twenty-one, and my father gave us written permission. Why should some stranger care? Give me a good reason!"

I was as irate as if I had the proverbial bee in my bonnet and demanded a suitable explanation.

"Girls have married GIs for a bread ticket. For the money. For the allotment check? Or, to become citizens. The CO has to check you out. Don't worry, Babe. It's nothing. He'll like you."

"First, I'm a federal civil service employee and earn more than you, remember? Second, I don't know what an allotment check is. Third, I was born in the sovereign state of New York. Fourth? It's nuts! I'm insulted. I don't have to meet this person, do I?"

"Yes. You have to. That is, you do if we're going to get married at Fort Belvoir."

"I thought you were free, white, and twenty-one! How come?"

"It's because of war brides. I think they caused it. Something like that. I'm unsure."

"Why me? I'm no war bride. I'm a native born American citizen! War brides are not. They are foreigners!"

"It's Army Regulations. If we want to get married, you have to be interviewed by my CO. Period. Not open for discussion. That's just the way it is. Regulations trump everything else."

Bill stuck out his lip in a little boy pout hoping he'd look pitiful and I'd relent, but I wasn't in a playful mood and when he tried to kiss me I pulled away and glared at him.

"Ah, come on, Babe. Don't be mad."

"Well? What *is* a CO? And why is our wedding any of his bees wax?"

I learned the acronym CO meant commanding officer. I couldn't understand why the CO had a say so. I crossed my arms tightly over my well endowed bosom and frowned.

"He's a nice guy. You'll like him. He acts 'in loco parentis,' in the absence of my parents. And he's a good dentist."

"A dentist? You're a combat veteran. It's stupid and I object. My father will object, and so will my mother. And she'll laugh at you, and at the CO and your stupid Army Regulations!"

I was furious, but Bill was adamant. No interview, no permission from the CO, no wedding. I could've argued to get married in Pennsylvania, but didn't. If Mister CO didn't approve me I'd suggest Pennsylvania and postpone the wedding until Christmas vacation. In fact, the more I thought about it the better I liked the idea of having our wedding in Lawrence Park where my relatives and old friends could all attend.

"Try to understand. I'm RA," Bill said. I didn't enquire what RA was. He repeated it. "I'm RA. That means Regular Army. I'm 'RA all the way' meaning I follow the Regs! It also means anyone who knows my RA number can find me anywhere. You should memorize it, Babe. Since we're getting married. But keep it to yourself."

I'm smart. I got it. "A" meant Army, but I pondered "R" meaning regular. Did that suggest there could be an "I" for irregular Army? I didn't dare ask. He appeared alternately dejected, angry and hopeful—like a little kid. I felt myself softening but tried to hide it.

"Okay. What's the number?"

"Right. My serial number is RA 14-34-51-93. Got it? It's sort of my personal identification number. Don't forget it. Now please go with me to meet my CO."

Against such logic what chance did a poor girl have? I mean, really? I burned that eight digit number into my memory and reluctantly went to meet the CO at the Belvoir dental clinic absolutely predetermined to dislike him, for no logical reason.

Being there made me feel like a slab of meat, a slave on the market, a lowly third-class criminal. I felt guilty like I should defend myself, but didn't know why. I asked myself: Wasn't I already found guilty of wanting to marry Bill for wrong reasons? The Constitution says innocent until proved guilty. Were my rights being violated?

I bit my tongue, checked my make-up in the rearview mirror, and holding my head high walked into the commanding officer's office, sat on the edge of the proffered seat, tried not to get white shoe polish on anything, and waited.

Fortunately, the interview went well but I needed multiple Band-Aides on my tongue to hide the wounds created by words bitten back and I remained livid, but I concealed it—a skill I would use a thousand times as an Army wife—and said nothing wrong and even smiled. The colonel was polite, friendly and jovial. Apparently satisfied that I wasn't a foreign spy or planning to steal from a poor lonely soldier he shook my hand, offered congratulations and said, "Permission to marry granted."

Well, Whoop-de-do, I thought, not realizing that just by being there I'd followed Army Regulations for the first of many times I would do so. Mister CO, colonel somebody, didn't know I intended to get married with, or without, his permission. Mentally, I stuck out my chewed up tongue, but didn't speak any disrespectful words. I was a disciplined young lady and my deportment was impeccable. But there wasn't an Army regulation against thinking. I could think anything, right? I admit to some shocking thoughts before I could relegate the incident to the deepest realms of memory.

Young GIs—government issued soldiers—can be seduced during wartime or any time by starving, desperate, opportunistic women anxious to become American citizens and willing to marry to achieve it. My contention is that that particular rule should not apply to employed, native born citizens, like me. I believe there should have been an exemption to the regulation, and in our case the necessity for me to be interviewed by the CO should have been waived. With the passage of time I finally understood the CO had no choice. He too, was bound by Army Regulations. He had to do it. Maybe he even agreed with me. Maybe he dreaded it as much as I. After all, in civilian life he was a dentist! What equipped a dentist to decide whether or not people should get married?

CHAPTER 5

— ✤ —

About Korea

THERE ARE MANY experts in the Army. Trained medics like the one who took my blood for the Wasserman test are highly valued on the battlefield and often risk their lives to treat patients. Bill said many medics were conscientious objectors. Those unarmed soldiers "are pretty special people who save lives nearly every day," he said.

"If they're highly trained like doctors to care for people, are medics real soldiers?"

"Well, hellfire, of course we're real soldiers! And we get scared, we bleed, and we die just like other soldiers. And we're brave. In fact, going into combat without a gun is scarier than knowing you at least have some way to defend yourself when they shoot at you. I had my fists and whatever I grabbed.

We're called support troops. We don't get many headlines in the papers because our mission is to *save*, not *take* lives. People aren't much interested hearing about that. After basic training at Fort Jackson I went to Texas for advanced training as a medic. In hand-to-hand? Medics do the best they can against an enemy with a gun and a bayonet. That's where my football experience with Coach Dave was a big help. I knew how to run and hit the ground rolling. Truth be told? When I had to, I fought dirty."

"Well, that sounds different. I had no idea. Did you have to kill anyone in Korea?"

"No, thank God. At least, I hope not...none that I know of... let's change the subject. Talk about something nice."

"One last question? What did you do with the wounded? Was there a hospital?"

"We loaded up ambulances and drove behind the lines to a hospital, if we could. We were a mobile Army surgical hospital, a MASH unit. And we took care of emergencies. Sometimes we sent them out on a whirlybird, other times we transported them in our ambulances. We just did quick fixes—triage—to separate the dead and dying.

Lots of guys died in Korea. Treated frostbite, too. At Chosin Reservoir—we called it Frozen Chosin—nobody got issued the right uniforms or boots. Thousands got frostbite. It was damn cold. Lost a lot of toes."

"That's terrible. I'm glad you didn't get shot or have frostbite. It sounds really awful. I don't know how you did all that."

"Yeah. Guys died from Chinese shells, Russian bullets, Korean guns, weather. Some froze to death. All I got was an ear infection. Still can't hear out of that ear."

"I was worrying about which gown to wear to the prom and who to go with while you were doing all that. You must think I'm terribly shallow!"

"War isn't all bad. In one way war is good, Babe. Good for civilians and good for the future. On the battlefield we learned a lot of stuff civilians benefit from when those doctors and medics return from the war. That's good, right? And, you aren't shallow, Babe, just a wee bit naïve."

"I mean you saw buddies blown to bits. How can that help civilians, or be good?"

"Surgical techniques, new medicines, how to do things speedier and save more lives is good. Right? Science moves fast in war, everything does. Scientists develop new cures much quicker. That's good, right?"

"That's amazing. I never thought of it that way before. You're amazing."

"Can we talk about something else, anything else but war? Like, when are you going to give this amazing guy some sugar?"

CHAPTER 6

— ✿ —

Are We There Yet?

My FIRST VISIT to the Land of Cotton wasn't what I expected. Actually, I didn't know what to expect. Without meaning to sound unkind it was rather like landing on Mars without a guide, a plan, or clear idea of what might happen.

Our honeymoon trip to Statesville began July fourth the morning after the wedding and following breakfast with Mother and Daddy at Howard Johnson's. Late the same day I met Bill's family and friends, most of whom claimed kinship to settlers and/or Bill's great-great-great-grandfather, Major William Gill, who rode with General George Washington. Ancestor worship was alive and well in Statesville in 1952—but excluded all Yankees like we don't exist.

Bill had shocked everyone by breaking with tradition and marrying a northerner—one they all agreed talked funny—and people wanted a glimpse of her. Some hadn't met a Yankee before but could discuss in graphic detail numerous crimes supposedly committed by Yankee *bluecoats* during what southerners refer to as the War of Northern Aggression or the War Between the States (1861-1865). They wondered how one of those "damnYankees"—one word, said like a swear word—tricked one of their popular bachelors into marriage and asked each other if I looked pregnant. Was that how he was hooked? If they only knew how he had pursued me!

I listened to Bill's drawl grow thicker and heard him trying to convince everyone I was "just wonderful," but most of all I observed him being treated like a small town hero and was impressed at how well liked and respected he was.

Naturally, some of the girls were curious and anxious to report what this person—the one calling herself Mrs. Gill—looked like. No doubt they were disappointed to see that Yankee wives look a lot like young southern matrons.

I didn't realize I would be on display and had chosen a brightly patterned simple cotton broomstick skirt, plain white blouse and old, brown huaraches in a sincere effort to fit in and not stand out— now I wished I had worn dressier clothes. As faces began to blur, and I couldn't remember their names, I mentioned to my new husband that I felt frumpy. Bill said I looked perfect. He insisted everyone was thrilled to welcome me. I wondered if the girl he'd lost to a civilian while he was away fighting a war might have been more than mildly curious, but I don't think I met her. I didn't see her picture either as that very day Bill destroyed all his old photos and said, "Let's forget the past, Babe."

While getting scrutinized, criticized, exorcised, and thoroughly welcomed I took him up on forgetting and let him get reacquainted with old friends while I daydreamed about breakfast that morning with Mother and Daddy.

Restaurants in Washington had been jam packed with vacationers but since my parents had stayed overnight at Howard Johnson's they were able to get us a table in the crowded dining room. I ordered cantaloupe. Bill admitted he'd never eaten cantaloupe but was willing to try it, since I was. I was nursing a second cup of coffee when Mother nudged Daddy and they stood up. It was time for them to begin the twelve hour drive to Erie. I hugged them and saw tears in his eyes when Daddy said good-bye.

I watched my parents drive away and heard Bill say it was "time to motor..." I had thought it was right—at the time—but later rued our short visit with my parents and the fact I, their only child, had sent them home so I could visit in-laws who hadn't even bothered to attend our wedding.

We headed south on Route #1 with the temperature nearing one hundred making me regret that I hadn't taken Bill's advice and worn shorts, but when he suggested hanging my feet out the window to catch a breeze I refused. I'd seen people do that and thought it was terribly low-class.

To pass the time I asked about his family, but Bill refused to answer and we sped past Alexandria in silence. Somewhere around Richmond, Virginia Bill spoke. "Statesville hasn't seen anything like you, Babe. They're going to really take notice when you wear that sexy, blue dress!"

My blue linen sheath was my favorite dress, but sexy? Mother and I called it Classic Greek style. I didn't plan to wear it in Statesville because I didn't want to stick out and be noticed. Bill just didn't understand; I wanted to fit in.

By noon the Buick had become an inferno. I wanted to stop, get something ice cold to drink, and postpone our trip to cooler weather, or maybe forever. Bill must have been hot, too. I felt the car glide to a stop and saw we were in the middle of nowhere beside an unpainted, dilapidated shack boasting a gas pump, air hose, a rusty sign advertising cold drinks, and kerosene for sale. Bill jumped out and was sprinting inside before I could say orange juice with ice. While waiting for his return I watched a Tabby cat claw at the screen door and saw it streak inside as Bill came running out carrying two small paper cups. When he approached the passenger side of the car I reached out through the open window to greedily accept the cold drink.

"Sorry, Babe. He's out of sodas, but he let us have these cups of ice."

Sodas? I thought about small round wrought iron and glass tables and chocolate ice cream with fizz water and whipped cream and a cherry on top—my favorite at Chacona's, a refectory in northwestern Pennsylvania.

"Sodas?" I said, eagerly tipping the cup to my lips.

"I wanted Nehi, but he said we're lucky to get scrapings from the bottom of the box."

Bottom of the box? No more of that ice would cross my lips, but I did rub some on my wrists. *Were we in the United States*? My face felt on fire. I pulled off my shoes and nylons, hiked up and waved my skirt and cotton petticoat and hoped to create a breeze.

Most cars weren't equipped with air conditioning in 1952. We traveled with the windows rolled down as dust and dry heat rolled in and steam rose from the black top. We passed strange looking fields of cracked red clay and a few tobacco barns, but no cities and no people. I began to wonder if we were lost. Where in the world was North Carolina? Had I trusted my life to a madman who couldn't even find it? I heard my stomach growling. Bill must have heard it, too.

"Getting hungry?" Bill hadn't spoken for several miles, nor had I.

"Yes. Very hungry." I felt better knowing we weren't going to have to starve to death.

"What would you like? Just name it, Babe."

"How about baked chicken, stuffing and gravy? That's my favorite," I said eagerly.

"I don't know. I meant did you want barbecue or a burger?"

"No. Uh-uh. Neither of those. Roasted chicken sounds good."

"Well, okay. We'll stop at the next place that's open, see if they have any."

We never found a restaurant and I stopped feeling hungry but grew apprehensive. What had I got myself into? Were there civilized people in North Carolina? Would snakes dangle from trees? What is Spanish moss? Would the girls be like Scarlet O'Hara? Would his mother like me? Was it much farther? Suddenly, I didn't want to visit Statesville, North Carolina. Especially, not on such a hot day. Maybe never!

"Can we go back to Arlington now?"

"You are kidding, right? We're almost there. In fact, look up ahead. See that car?"

CHAPTER 7

— ❧ —

South of Familiar

Bill pulled onto the berm and left the motor running.

"What are we doing?" I said, panic rising in my throat.

"Get out, honey. Ride with them the rest of the way."

Could I have heard wrong? Get out? Ride with strangers? To where? The other car was parked on the opposite side of the road, but facing us. Who were they? Why was I getting out? Had I been tricked? Daddy had been right! He always warned me against being so trusting. I'd trusted Master Sergeant W. T. Gill and look what that got me!

Clutching my purse to my breast I stepped from the car onto the tarry, black road prepared to run fast until I found a house or a store with a pay phone. I'd call Daddy collect and he'd call the cops to rescue me. Then, he'd do a thing or two about this situation! You could bet your bottom dollar on that!

Right before Daddy walked me down the aisle—was it only last night? Anyway, he had said to let him know if Bill didn't treat me right. Well, I certainly was going to tell him that as soon as we arrived in this godforsaken place Bill had tried to trade me to white-slavers and smiled while doing it!

I saw a desolate road stretching in both directions and should have screamed and run, but I stood there looking from one car to the other and all around. Trees lined both sides of the two lane macadam without a building in sight. My hopes of rescue evaporated. More angry than afraid, I narrowed my eyes at Bill. He grinned back like Alice's Cheshire. What was happening? That was an odd reaction, even for him.

A middle-age man crossed the road to the other side of Bill's car. He leaned in the open window. Did he have a gun? Was it a hold up? Was he buying me? Had I been sold? What was going on?

"Hey, son! How was the trip? Good. Y'all follow me now, you hear? Don't worry. We'll take good care of her. See you at home."

I saw he wore a white short-sleeve shirt and clean, neat trousers and was very tanned. He was about the same size as Bill but had curly salt and pepper hair instead of dark hair cut very short like Bill's. I watched him turn and walk straight toward me, beefy arms outstretched the way Daddy's were whenever I ran to him for a gigantic hug.

I managed a timid "Hello?" Before I could say anything more he grabbed and hugged me. Was this man possibly Bill's own father?

"Oof," I said as he put me down.

"You come along with me, now. You heah? Billy'll be comin' right smart."

That's how I met Mister Gill. Chagrined and without a backward glance I climbed into the back seat of his nice new Dodge. After a big "He-haw" and a U-turn, and like a bat out of Hell, he sped back the way they'd come. I hoped my husband of less than one entire day was behind us.

A dark haired woman wearing a lot of jewelry, long sleeves, and bright red lipstick sat in the front. I wondered who she was. Too young to be Bill's mother, I thought. And then she spoke.

"Hello. My name is Grace," she said.

That didn't tell me much about who she was. I wondered how I could escape from this mess, but I also thought about Sunday school and the story of Ruth and Naomi and remembered these words: wither thou goest, I will go...and thy people shall be my people....I decided I had just met Bill's people. I'm pragmatic. I settled into the buttery soft leather and said hello to Grace, whoever she might be.

In the time it took to come to this decision we arrived at a freshly painted white bungalow its manicured lawn currently decorated with parked cars. People came out of the house and waved cheerily as we pulled up. I played follow the leader onto the tiny porch and entered a small living room where I couldn't take my eyes off the highly polished bare floor. I'd never seen a room without wall-to-wall carpet or a living room that didn't have a six foot long sofa, or any sofa at all.

Chairs were dragged in from other parts of the house and we managed to sit in a large lopsided circle. Introductions followed. When Bill arrived chatter stopped to wait for him to sit beside me. After a few moments of silence somebody spoke up addressing me with such a thick drawl I had to strain to understand.

She said, "Say something in Yankee."

Thank God, Bill rescued me before I could put my foot in my mouth. Everyone accepted whatever Bill did and it became immediately obvious that Bill was a VIP.

"Excuse us," he said, propelling me with one hand on my elbow. Nobody tried to stop us as we toured his father's house and walked straight through the kitchen and screened back porch out into the yard. It was a great escape, and in the nick of time, before I could disgrace myself by laughing out loud at the ludicrous request to speak Yankee. It had been a genuine serious, innocent request, but still laughable.

"I figured you were feeling a little overwhelmed in there. Better now?"

"Yes. Thanks for rescuing me. What's the name of this street your people live on?"

"Salisbury Road. Give me a kiss."

"Salisbury? Like the steak? Stop that. Somebody will see us."

"Steak? I don't know. I said give me a kiss, but a hug will do for now. See that house t'other side of the dirt road, up yonder? A good ole neggra family lives there. Known them 'bout just forever. We save left-overs for them. You might've thought we're prejudiced here in the south. Proves we aren't. The slop bucket's on the back porch, case you need to know."

Slop bucket! You give leftovers to the neighbors? This is supposed to be nice?

"You should recall I'm part Negro! On The Leonard side! Remember? Don't let my blonde hair and blue eyes fool you."

Slop bucket charity! Disgusting! My lie was taking on a life of its own with strange experiences popping up unpredictably, and unexpected circumstances, like right now.

"Yeah, I'm high yeller! You better remember that, buster!"

Bill looked stunned, but recovered quickly. He pulled me into his arms and whispered. "I don't care what color you are." I saw Grace standing there and knew she heard what we said, but she pretended she didn't and insisted we should go back inside the house with her.

We'd been married one whole day. I had ventured to a place where I felt like Alice down the rabbit hole and didn't know what might happen next. It was an exhausting twenty hours and I was ready for bed. Or was I? Where would we sleep? Was that the next surprise? I began mentally picturing rooms. It was a cute little house, but it only had two bedrooms.

One was reserved for Mister Gill and his wife, Grace. The other was occupied by Grace's daughter, Sonja, and Grace's mother—called "Tube Rose Annie" because of the Tube Rose chawing ta'backy she favored. There wasn't an attic or basement.

Did Bill know where we'd sleep? Certainly not in the living room where there wasn't even a sofa. Hopefully, not in the car. There must be a hotel in Statesville! Maybe?

After the last guest had gone and we said goodnight all around I still didn't know where I would sleep. Bill led me to what had once been a garage. It smelled musty. I saw stacked cartons, a chiffonier, and an old bed with a double mattress that sagged to the middle.

"Before I joined the Army this was my room. Hasn't been used since. Reckon now it's sort of a storage room. We can sleep here and have some privacy away from the others." He stripped quickly and climbed into bed naked motioning for me to join him.

"We're both exhausted, Mrs. Gill. Get some shut-eye."

In seconds he was sound asleep. Before my body gave in to oblivion I heard my mother's voice saying: You made your bed, Suzie-Q. Now, go to sleep in it.

I woke up alone in a large room that stunk of mildew. Where was I? Where was Bill? Then I remembered. I was in the converted garage-storage-bedroom on Salisbury Road and the little girl standing beside the bed staring at me was Sonja. I sat up and pulled the sheet to my chin.

"I'm glad he married you instead of Maxine," she said.

"Maxine? Who's Maxine?" I was wide awake now.

"A girl everybody said he'd marry. Both families thought so. How come he married you instead? Did he have permission?"

"Well, yes. He had permission. Now if you'll hand me that robe, I'll get up."

"Billy's gone to the Texaco station with his daddy. Mama's at work. But Grannie and me are here. I'll fix your breakfast. Billy said fix anything you want."

"You?' You fix breakfast?"

"I'm almost twelve years old. Of course I do. What do you want?"

"How about orange juice?"

"Uh, we don't have that."

"Okay. A piece of toast will be fine. Can you do that?"

"Not exactly. Uh, we don't exactly have a toaster."

"Coffee? No milk or sugar. Can you do that?"

"Yes! Want a country ham biscuit with it?"

Sonja politely waited for me to answer. But what was a country ham biscuit? It was my turn to wonder how to respond. I'd never eaten, or even heard of, a country ham biscuit and made a mental note to ask my husband the difference between city ham and country ham.

"Well, no thanks. I guess just black coffee, please."

The kitchen was large. I sat at an oilcloth covered table and sipped instant coffee while Sonja filled me in on who was who, and what I could expect to happen that day.

"You'll have to go have dinner with his mother, Eva. Billy knows that. She's already phoned here twice this morning. It'll be at noon, you know. Then you'll probably go meet Granny—the other one— and Mama and Bob, that's Billy's daddy, are taking you out to eat steak tonight."

"That's a full day. I'll have to wait to wash my hair until tomorrow morning."

"Oh, no! You can't do that. Tomorrow's Sunday! That'd be a big, big sin."

"Sin? I have to work Monday." She looked so stricken I told her I'd reconsider.

I wandered into the living room in time to see Grace's mother expertly spit tobacco juice into an empty coke bottle. The sight made me gag. I turned on my heel, retreated to the bedroom, packed my clothes, and thought of my maternal grandmother. She must be spinning in her grave if she knows I married a descendent of her father's sworn enemy—a Johnnie Reb--and because of what Annie had just done. Yuck! I could imagine Grandmother Leonard's harsh words of disgust and in my mind's eye pictured her pursed lips and disapproving frown. I sat down on the lumpy bed and bit my lip, determined not to cry. *Stiff upper lip, pip, pip and all that,* I told myself. Life in Bill's world certainly wasn't boring. Would that be enough?

Bill's nonsense whistle and a whiff of Old Spice after shave followed the sound of his shoes slapping against the bare wood in the living room. He bounded into the bedroom smiling and didn't seem to notice how straight my back was, or the packed suitcase at my feet.

"Hel-lo, sugah! You look mighty cute sitting there on the bed waiting. What are you waiting for?" He leered at me. "I bet I know!" he added stepping out of his pants.

"Not that, you idiot. Where have you been? I don't even speak the same language the natives do. Don't you dare go off again and leave me here alone."

"Sure, honey. I'm sorry. But if I promise that, it will cost you a sloppy big kiss."

Ignoring him I said, "Sonja says I can't wash my hair tomorrow because it's Sunday."

"Well, yeah. Blue laws. Bible belt. Nobody does anything on Sunday. Isn't it that way where you come from?" Pennsylvania's taverns closed, but I shook my head. It was only thirty miles to New York State and Kelly's Tavern and they were always open.

"What should I do? I don't want to cause a problem, but I need to wash my hair."

"Wash your hair early on Sunday, Babe. But you'll have to dry it in the breezes 'cause we're heading out at zero five hundred (five a.m.). We have to get back to Arlington before supper time and you have to go to work Monday morning. Right? We have to get home and to bed early," Bill said.

"That's why I wanted to do it today, or Sunday. But we're going too many places today so I guess it will be Sunday. Sonja also mentioned a certain Maxine? Do you know anybody by that name? And not the Maxine your cousin dates. A different one."

"She's just a girl I know. Her folks? Well, they might've thought we'd get together."

The rest of our Fourth of July holiday—honeymoon—quickly passed. I did find time to explain to Sonja about being required to earn the colonel's approval and needing *his* permission before we could get married at Fort Belvoir. She didn't understand any more than I had.

"I'm underage in Pennsylvania," I told her. "I needed daddy's written permission, but Bill, being a soldier had to get permission from the commanding officer instead of his father."

"Why? Billy's almost twenty-three an' that's way old enough to get married. Mama was only 'bout thirteen when I was born. I know a girl from school? She got hitched in Rock Hill with nobody's permission and she was just fourteen. Billy? Needing permission? That's plain stupid, and I don't like it," she added.

Clearly Sonja adored her step-brother and felt defensive.

"Neither did I, but we had to do it. And it's okay, Sonja. It's Army Regulations. Between you and me, I thought it was stupid, and it made me mad, but we did it."

Cleanliness is next to godliness. Sunday morning while it was still dark and the household slept I moved very quietly and tiptoed into the only bathroom, washed my hair, and wrapped a babushka around my sinfully sopping wet head not caring that it made me look like an immigrant peasant just getting off the boat at Ellis Island.

As we entered Salisbury Road and pulled away from a driveway full of people waving farewell the sun had barely sneaked above a tall, white steeple in downtown Statesville. I spun the dial on the radio hoping to find a news station, but it was Burl Ives singing about a big Rock Candy Mountain. I hummed along with Burl as we sped north.

"Hey! Honey? What are you, Babe? A redneck? Turn off the hillbilly crap."

"Okay," I said wondering what a redneck was. "But, actually, I like country music. And I like this song. Don't you?"

"Nope."

I turned the radio off and stared out the window thinking about everything that had happened since boarding a Greyhound bus only four weeks ago. I started a Civil Service job, married Bill, and visited Statesville to meet his people. What a whirlwind! I hadn't had much time to think about it until now, but I recalled each of Sonja's questions, thought about the night at the Fort Belvoir swimming pool, and smiled about the blind date arranged by Nancy. Whew! I was exhausted just thinking about it!

The next time Bill spoke I was reminiscing about how conveniently time stood still or we might not have been married at all. My parents rode to the ceremony with me because Daddy didn't know the way to Fort Belvoir. On the way to the eight o'clock (twenty hundred hours) wedding I took a wrong turn and we arrived twenty minutes late. I feared Bill would have given up on me and left the chapel. We never could explain it but that night Bill's watch had stopped and he didn't know I was late! I also remembered Daddy was as nervous as a first sergeant waiting for the Inspector General and kept asking me which foot I wanted to start on, but we made it down the aisle okay and he managed to give me away. By twenty-one hundred hours, with my parents and a few friends present, for better or worse, I became an Army wife.

I was still thinking about all that when Bill startled me back to the present. "We'll grab chow 'round 'bout Ruffin, or Danville, Virginia. Okay, Babe?"

"Sure."

It sounded like he'd said, Rough Inn. Much later I learned that Ruffin—not Rough Inn as I'd thought I heard--is a North Carolina city near the Virginia line, but we didn't stop there.

CHAPTER 8

The Visit

MY HAIR DRIED quickly and before we reached Danville I had brushed out the pin curls and put away the scarf getting ready to stop to eat some place, but we didn't stop until we pulled in at a gas station in Arlington. Then we went to the Hot Shoppe and I ate my favorite fruit salad with orange sherbet, fresh hot rolls with honey-butter and sipped on a milkshake while Bill consumed a hamburger, French fries, and glasses of sweet ice tea.

A month later we received unexpected visitors. One evening after supper we heard a knock at the door. I hurried to open it thinking it might be Nancy, but four friends of my merchant marine former boyfriend crowded the doorway and spilled into the hall.

"What are *you* doing here?" I asked quietly, so I wouldn't alarm my husband.

"You know who sent us. He can't believe you really married somebody else."

"Well, I am married. Daddy put it in the Erie newspaper. Is that how he found out?"

"Nope, but that's how we knew your address. When he came home from Lorraine, Ohio he had a diamond ring and planned to pop the question. I told him what I read in the paper. His sister, Doris, is pretty mad at you right now."

"Oh. That's bad. I'm sorry. He deserved better. Come in for a minute and meet Bill."

Bill was only four years their senior but an adult. He looked a bit angry—or jealous. Maybe both. The room filled with testosterone tension in spite of Bill's thinly veiled attempt to display southern charm and be a polite host.

Brad said they'd be in town several days and he planned to call me the next day. I wrote down the number for the switchboard at my office. "See you tomorrow," he said. I thought *oh, no. you won't. I had seen the expression on my husband's face and knew what I had to do.*

As soon as I arrived at the office the next morning I made an excuse to talk with Ellen, our young boy-crazy file clerk. She was in the file room alone, as usual. Everybody knew she dated soldiers, sailors, or airman and liked to tell us where she went on those dates. I entered the file room and closed the door. Did she have a rule against dating civilians? I hoped not.

My boss, a handsome, young naval officer originally from Baltimore, had asked me to keep a list of which branch of the military she favored, but Ellen was an equal opportunity dater. He was flabbergasted by her stamina, or something. Anyway, he asked her to report to me first thing each day and I kept a log. So far every date had been with a member of the military. I leaned against the door holding it shut so we could talk without interruption, crossed my fingers for luck, and explained about my former boyfriend's sleuthing buddies.

"I need your help," I said after answering questions about their visit. "I'm afraid they'll hang around and come to see me again. Bill tried to be polite last night, but if they return I'm afraid he won't. Will you help me? Do you have three girlfriends who'd like to go out on the town dancing and the works? Maybe you could get souvenirs and photos, too. Spend their money on champagne and send them back to Pennsylvania for good?"

"Yeah. Sure. Who with?"

Maybe I shouldn't have done it, but it was too late to back out.

"Think about this. You could take three friends clubbing, spend *allllll* their money—empty their wallets, and tell them to go home and stay there. Okay?"

I hoped Ellen and her girlfriends would send the spies back home right away.

"Oh, sure. Yeah. I get it. That's a great plan. Sure. I can do it."

"Can you do it tonight? Have fun and be sure they're broke before you leave them?"

"You're on," she said. "We'll do it. Thanks. You're a doll. You set it up when that guy calls, but don't say where I live. Tell him to meet us tonight at Lincoln Memorial, nine sharp. Thanks, again. Oh, and tell your boss I said to add Marines—big ones--to the log book!"

When Brad called I asked if he'd like to meet some local girls and have a good time.

Credit cards and ATMs were far in the future. The guys all had jobs and some money, but it was a cash society and they had meager funds. I told Bill that Brad and the others had gone home but I didn't say how I knew or mention Ellen's name.

"I guess he was a nice guy. Regret not waiting for him?" Bill was still a little jealous.

"No-no-no. But I feel bad about not telling him before his buddies did. It happened so fast—us getting married—and all. I didn't know how to reach him." I guess I looked forlorn. I was feeling a bit rotten because I had hurt an old friend the way I had.

"Come here, Babe. Give me a kiss and let me make you feel all better."

⚭

At the last minute on Christmas Eve we decided to drive to Pennsylvania and spend the holiday with my folks. It was very late and snowing as we hurried north on old, narrow, winding roads because I-77 didn't exist yet. Bill's obsession to lead extended to hazardous driving conditions including whiteouts in the Appalachian Mountains. I knew we weren't equipped for snow survival, but my husband was a risk taker, sure of our invincibility, and confident we wouldn't get stranded in a storm. As we passed dark houses with twinkling Christmas lights I looked in vain for signs of people.

"This will get worse. Let's stop," I said, wiping fog from my window with a red woolen mitten and turning up the heater.

"I know what I'm doing, Babe. Korea had snow and was as cold as a witch's tit."

From years of experience I knew new snow covered old ice. I strained to see the road in a starless night, but it was camouflaged by falling snow and visibility was zero.

"It's pretty dark out there. Can you actually see where the road ends and fields begin? I know I can't."

"Sure. Sit tight. Relax. If you get cold, snuggle up closer. This is nothing, Babe. In a bit we'll be coming to the Pennsylvania Turnpike. I've got it under control."

No, you do not, mister. If you did, you'd pull in at the next house you see and go pound on their door until they let us in. So you saw a few snowflakes in Korea, big deal!

Our Buick slid across the road swan diving into a ditch. I looked behind us. What I saw made me sit up and cheer. I wanted to jump up and down and yell hallelujah. A huge, yellow snowplow plodded up the highway behind us. My excitement was brief. Bill gunned the engine rocking the car back and forth. Suddenly, with a mighty backward lurch, we spun back onto the road miraculously turned in the right direction.

"Didn't you see the plow? He'll be here in a minute. Aren't we waiting for it?"

The car's engine roared. I made a mental note to learn the medical term for grinding my molars, something I was doing so I wouldn't say words I might later regret.

"Nah. Not waiting. We've gotta move out. If he wants, that ole boy can follow us."

I was shocked into silence. We barely spoke for the rest of the trip. But we arrived safely and in time for Christmas morning breakfast with my parents. I didn't tell Daddy that Bill led the plow up the Turnpike or how much I dreaded the ride back to D.C. I did tell my mother that her southern son-in-law drove in snow like he *thought* he knew what he was doing.

"Interesting," she replied. I knew she understood. "Why don't you drive?"

"Since we got married? Bill does the driving. He says if I drive it wakes him up."

♋

Bill received overseas orders in January and by March I knew I was pregnant. I returned to Pennsylvania to wait for him to send for me to join him in Germany. I would need a passport. One warm morning Mother went with me to the court house. I didn't have a birth certificate. Oddly, neither did she, but my luck held. The clerk let Mother raise her right hand and swear I was a natural born citizen from New York State and that she had been present at my birth and was over the age of sixteen at the time. (she was thirty) My passport was issued. Now I only had to wait for the baby to be old enough to travel.

Every July for 100 years The Hodges Family held a big reunion, but in July of 1953 it was Mother's first time to be the hostess and she didn't want anything spoiling it. Balmy breezes kissed white-caps on Lake Erie making it an ideal day for swimming, boating, picnics, sunbathing, or playing on the beach. One or two puffy white clouds dotted a lapis lazuli sky completing a postcard perfect scene as we waited for late arrivals to come from Cleveland and Ashtabula, Ohio.

In the middle of the afternoon I felt strange and went inside our rented cottage fearing something was wrong with the baby. In fact, I felt certain. When I told Mother I was concerned she said, "Nah. Everything's fine." I suspected she didn't really believe that because she immediately went away to canvass older ladies.

When she returned she said, "Nothing to worry about."

I didn't care what a bunch of octogenarians said. Something was wrong. I knew it. I wanted to see my doctor, but we were thirty miles from the city and I didn't have a car.

"It's Sunday, honey. He won't be there. If you insist, we'll go first thing Monday."

CHAPTER 9

—— ⚹ ——

Ships Ahoy!

WHILE I EXPERIENCED a difficult pregnancy in Pennsylvania without him, my husband was being wined, dined, and bribed in Germany. New friends treated him like a celebrity until he adamantly refused to provide coffee, sugar, nylons, etc. for them to sell on the black market. Bill, a Regular Army noncommissioned officer sent to help occupy the region until sovereignty would be returned in 1955, distanced himself from all foreign nationals except Shorty, a cute German girl who worked at the Dental Clinic.

Soldiers who witnessed the unspeakable carnage that took place during Hitler's reign of terror were replaced with a smattering of fresh, but seasoned soldiers, and thousands of green troops. Many of these replacements had been psyched up and trained to kill, but now they were being instructed to make friends. Making friends with the enemy hadn't been part of basic training. As their boots sloshed through unchartered waters soldiers trained to be lean, mean killing machines—suddenly ambassadors of goodwill—lacked the necessary training to know what to do. This caused enormous confusion and people on both sides became wary.

Behaving more like teenagers away from home for the first time many young soldiers forgot how to conduct themselves in a strange land, among people they didn't trust or understand, surrounded by irresistible temptations and with pockets full of cash. The rate of exchange gave them a spending power of four to one making it easy to eat dinner in a nice restaurant for about fifty cents of American money.

They were like kids let loose in a candy store. If the cadre didn't keep them busy they drank too much, whored too much, and fought with each other. Consequently, artillery and infantry troops spent most of their time on training exercises out in the field several miles away from cities, civilian populations, and temptation.

൭

Meanwhile, I had been in Pennsylvania joyfully anticipating the birth of our first child and excited because I knew the three of us would move into an apartment in Bavaria to begin the "happily ever after" phase in a few weeks. As spring flowed into summer I counted the days until baby would be six weeks old and we could leave for overseas. That was the plan. But my carefully made plans were eradicated, travel was postponed, and I wouldn't be taking Richard with me when I went.

There are no rules for facing the death of a child, but I learned there are rules about almost everything else and Bill had his own rules, too. Most of all he studied and memorized military rules and regulations and followed them. I found some to be really confusing. I asked about hurry up and wait.

"Hurry up and wait? Sure. That's normal," he said matter-of-factually.

Oh, really? I believed being forced to wait was rude and contradictory to another primary military rule: Be punctual, on time, or a little early. There also were rules about housekeeping. I agreed with most of them, but when the children arrived it wasn't easy to achieve his superlative demands. Bill had high cleanliness standards, but unlike most husbands he was willing to help keep our kids and quarters clean. One day I had a suggestion.

"I have an idea! Can't the privates haave a GI party here (a cleaning party) Friday night, like at the clinic?"

My question was unanswered except for a discourteous finger, which I ignored, waved in my direction. I tried to keep our home inspection ready—paint it, hide it, or toss it out.

Once, when we lived in an apartment in Langley Park, Maryland, in 1956, I went overboard trying to meet or surpass Bill's impossibly high expectations. I should say impossibly high standards that nobody else even tried to follow! For example, I crawled on my hands and knees and used a paring knife to remove specks of dirt from cracks between the polished floor boards. I was still very young, but that was crazy, and I was nuts to do it. Bill had no complaints about my housekeeping. Why should he?

After I resigned from MSA we moved several times and I missed my friends, but Bill had an ironclad rule about making new friends. I didn't like that rule. I was lonely and his rule was unworkable. The rule: don't make friends from the clinic, or the battalion, or neighbors. I thought, *wait a minute.*

"Who does that leave?" A shrug ended that conversation.

No deal. I won't agree. I knew that rule was ridiculous and unenforceable. He expected me to obey and didn't notice when I ignored his ultimatum and began making friends wherever I could. I was limited to knowing people I could meet nearby. That meant I befriended neighbors.

I managed to make quick friendships with other Army wives and learned about other parts of the world like Kyoto, London, Moscow and cities all over the USA, but when I tried sharing that with my mother she saw it as problematic. Never one to mince words—a tradition she learned from relatives from Vermont--she suggested the reason I made Army friends so fast was because misery loves company. Ouch!

We moved often. Keeping long time relationships became difficult, but I did have a few. A happy life requires friends and most doctors and pastors will agree that having a friend is good for us, but having a loyal and true friend in troubled times is more than that. It's a blessing.

⚘

On that unforgettable, hot day at the Hodges Reunion in July 1953 I needed a friend who'd believe it when I said my baby—my precious Richard—died. Nobody at the reunion believed me. They acted like they thought I didn't know anything. But true to her word the next morning Mother drove me into town to see the doctor.

He was only a GP, young and inexperienced. He offered to find out what we should do since he hadn't been able to hear a heartbeat. It was obvious he didn't believe me.

"I'll discuss your case at the hospital board meeting and ask OB/GYN specialists for advice. When the time's right I'll call Red Cross and get your husband back home."

"No. Please don't contact the Red Cross. Why would you? He's three thousand miles away. It's too late for him to do anything." *Why aren't you listening? My baby already is dead!*

"Don't worry. I'll take care of it. He'll come home. You need him here."

Why? I've cried buckets for our loss already. Let him stay in Germany and let me have a ticket so I can join him there. He wasn't listening to me.

"No. Don't. I don't want that." I repeated it to no avail.

The OB/GYN specialists advised us to wait because it's safer, they deemed, for the mother to let nature take its course. My doctor said we'd do that and not induce labor.

Daddy said, "Poppycock." He continued to worry and wring his hands.

Five weeks later, September 7th 1953, I arrived at Hamot Hospital in labor only to be told Daddy had to sign for me before our baby was delivered because I wasn't old enough to sign for myself!

The nurses felt sorry for me because Richard had died and Bill was overseas. Two days later on my twentieth birthday they brought me a cake with candles and we celebrated in the maternity ward while Daddy made all the burial arrangements before arriving to take me home.

The phone was ringing when we arrived. It was a transatlantic call via ham radio operators. I sobbed the entire three minutes after Bill said he was on the way home.

A month after that tearful phone call Bill finally showed up. In my mind I reviewed the things he had missed and thought about my Swedish paternal grandfather, Fabian. He had sailed here from Sweden on the passenger ship Romeo seventy-five years earlier and arrived in America in the same length of time—thirty days.

"What took you so long? I had about given up on you."

"I got to the port city of Bremerhaven a few hours after we spoke but I had to sit there and wait for an MSTS going to CONUS. That's a bad example of "hurry up and wait." But I'm here now. How's about a kiss, Babe? I've come a long way. Don't I deserve a big ole sloppy kiss?"

A cottage cheese and fruit diet had already taken off the baby fat. Bill thought I was slim, soft and cuddly, but like most Army wives I had an inner strength as durable and strong as Pittsburgh steel, and I was resilient. Facing Rickard's death without Bill had made me even stronger.

I had packed away all the baby things and survived the empty arms syndrome like other parents do—by pushing down the pain and pretending everything was just hunky-dory. After Bill arrived Richard's death was seldom mentioned. Maybe the baby seemed unreal which would explain why he behaved like he was on a holiday instead of an emergency furlough. Or perhaps it had to do with what he had seen in Korea—maybe he had not known what to say to me-- what to do. For whatever reason, we spent our time doing fun things. We saw movies, swam and sun-bathed at the Golf Course beach, went horseback riding in Cook's Forest, and pretended everything was okay.

As leaves began to turn red, gold, and orange, Bill said his furlough was up and it was time to resume his role of oceangoing hitchhiker. I rode with him on the New York Central as far as Buffalo and took the next passenger train back to Erie while he went on to New York City to wait for a military ship heading to Europe.

A few days later he called to say he wanted me to join him in New York. That was a surprise and I asked why.

"Yeah, believe it or not, it's lonely here, Babe. And I miss you. New York is a big place. But you pick the spot. I'll find you."

"Really? In that case, meet me at the New York City YWCA."

"Well, I'm not actually in *that* city. It's close to New York City, just across the state line. I'm by New Brunswick, New Jersey."

"But where's that near? I never heard of that place."

"It's near Fort Dix. I'll ship out of Dix when I go. I think it's the nearest town to Dix."

"Okay. Find me at the Young Women's Christian Association, the YW, in New Brunswick. I'll find that, and you find me tomorrow after lunch."

I had been participating in "Y" activities since I was eight years old. Bill had never seen a "Y" and knew nothing about them. I had a childish faith that all cities had a residential YWCA and YMCA, just like Erie. I assured him there had to be a "Y" in New Brunswick. Fortunately, we were lucky. New Brunswick had a YWCA—not a very active one-- but I was prepared to wait there facing the door until Bill came. I didn't wait long.

"Surprise!" Bill said kissing me passionately.

Nobody cared about the impropriety, except me. A few people even applauded, but I was embarrassed. He grabbed my luggage, smiled and saluted everyone in the "Y" as we left. Then we started down the street hand-in-hand looking for a taxi.

It was easy to recognize Bill was a soldier. He was required to wear his dress uniform with the "Ike" jacket, but his demeanor, walk and haircut, were dead giveaways, too. We went to the USO and got tickets to see Cab Calloway. A taxi driver directed us to 42nd and Broadway and told us about the Automat. We entertained ourselves by dropping coins into slots and opening little glass doors to choose our supper. Passersby greeted us respectfully calling him Sarge, Master Sergeant, or Top.

On the way to Radio City we gawked at ourselves on television in a store window and attended a radio give away show where they asked for a serviceman to be a contestant but no amount of urging convinced Bill to volunteer. Later we admired the "Big Apple" from the top of the Empire State building.

We couldn't afford to stay overnight in the city and spent our last dime on roasted chestnuts in Central Park before returning to our sleazy hotel room in New Jersey. Bill shoved a big dresser against the flimsy door. I hadn't been afraid until I saw the wicked looking knife he stuck in the doorjamb and another dangerous blade protruding from under Bill's pillow.

"How come you couldn't have waited in Erie, instead of this hellhole?"

"My thirty day furlough was up. I had to report in at Dix by a certain hour, or be AWOL. There hasn't been a MSTS (military sea transport ship) leaving CONUS this week, but I'm on stand by and have to wait right here, in case there's a change."

"I get the AWOL part. Everyone knows what that means, but CONUS?"

"CONUS? That's what we call The United States. CON-tinental-US. CONUS. Get it?"

The next day Bill helped me climb aboard the bus and seated mere minutes before double whoosh sounds closed two pneumatic doors and the Greyhound moved away from the curb with Bill aboard. In a loud voice the driver announced it was okay for Bill to "ride along a ways." I guess he had to walk back to Fort Dix.

CHAPTER 10

❧

The Blue Coat

MY MONTHLY ALLOTMENT check, which was partly from Bill's paycheck and part from the government, came to about $150.00. It was barely enough for necessities and our New York trip had taken all my money. I was flat broke. On the ride to Erie I thought about getting a job to earn enough to pay for passage on an ocean liner. Otherwise, I would have to wait until military family housing was constructed before the Army would send me overseas at government expense. I didn't want to wait.

I found a job as switchboard operator in a private hospital near my parents' house. One afternoon a nun stopped at my desk on her way out and, and like I did for others, I handed her the bill for her procedure. A few minutes passed before the doctor in charge stormed out yelling loudly enough for everybody hear.

"What's wrong with you! We don't charge for services if the patient is a nun!"

Really? Why not? Where is that in my employee handbook?

"Sorry. I didn't know. It won't happen again," I said.

Dr. K. stomped back inside his office and shut the door.

I spent my first paycheck at Lucy's in Jamestown where I made the mistake of buying a light blue full-length coat with a big silver fox collar. How chic I would look in Paris! I didn't realize in postwar Germany such a stylish coat would mark me as a boastful, uncaring, ugly American. Women I would meet there might want, but couldn't have, such finery. Once I understood the coat made me look like a show-off I felt so embarrassed I refused to wear it until we returned Stateside.

Being a clerk/switchboard operator in a small hospital run by a doctor—who in my opinion was a bit odd—wasn't as easy as it sounds, but the hours were good and I could walk home for lunch. The other staff members were nice, but it was a hostile work environment. Nevertheless, I worked hard until I had enough to pay Cunard Lines for a one-way ticket to Le Harve, France. Then I happily quit that job.

CHAPTER 11

— ✂ —

FMD

MOTHER HAD GIVEN me the steamer trunk she used when she was a student at Battle Creek College in Michigan and I was in my room debating what to pack in it when Daddy walked in looking sad and down in the dumps. He was mumbling about our relatives who emigrated from Sweden before I was even born.

"I'll never see my little girl again," he moaned. "Two weeks from now you'll be gone. I know you gotta, but I don't gotta like it!"

"Daddy, don't. This is different. It's only three years. I'll be back before you know it. I promise."

"That's what they all say. Pa swore he would, too. Nobody crosses the pond both ways. It's a big ocean. You get to the other side? You stay."

"Honest, Daddy. We'll be back." I tried to convince him, but his mind was set.

The second week of January in 1954 I said adieu to Erie and sailed from New York City's Pier Eight-five aboard the USS United States, the fastest and newest luxury liner in the world. Shipboard dining was elegant, my state-room on "A" deck was lovely, the service was excellent, and we made the crossing to France in record time.

At customs a guard recognized my green passport as USA, waved me on, and pointed to the crowded Le Harve to Paris boat-train shuttle. I climbed aboard and found a seat in a compartment with four American airmen and an attractive young woman about my age. I didn't let on that I spoke English and allowed them to assume I was French.

A short time later I opened the compartment door to follow a narrow aisle the length of the car as the train swayed and weaved down the track to Paris. I had to stand in the aisle and wait my turn only to discover it was a unisex toilet so small that once inside I could barely turn around.

The Paris train station lacked the familiar redcaps who had helped me with my luggage in New York City. I watched in horror as passengers began tossing their belongings out the windows onto the tracks at the enormous depot. If I followed that example would I ever see my suitcases again?

Presented with no choices, and thinking about my high school history teacher, Mister Poly, who said, "When in Rome do as the Romans" I copied the other passengers then hurried off the train. Naturally, I had not thrown out the handtooled, leather shoulder strap bag containing my passport, lipstick, comb, threaded needle, and change of panties. I knew my steamer trunk would be delivered later, but I had tossed new outfits and several of my favorite belongings doubtful I would find them again!

Paris was famous for the arts and is a lovely city but also one of the most dangerous places in the world for a young woman traveling alone. My cash—called greenbacks—remained securely pinned to my slip in a small velvet pouch Grandmother Leonard had given me. I wasn't afraid, but cautious. Since I was a child Daddy had drummed into me the importance of looking around my surroundings and keeping an escape route in mind. I tried to do that while racing across multiple train tracks following other travelers always wondering if they knew what they were doing. I looked up and saw a trestle sporting ugly graffiti that read:

Yankee Go Home. And then, to my surprise, when I turned around Bill was there and had collected my suitcases.

We stayed overnight in a hotel in the heart of Paris. The next day we visited The Louvre and marveled at the former royal palace on the Seine that had become a famous art museum. It was there on the steps that I learned even soldiers can be shocked, and Bill was. A vendor approached him and tried to sell him photos of nude women in lewd positions. He couldn't believe it happened at a world famous art museum—especially not when I was standing with him—and it made him angry.

We ate lunch in a small cafe on the Rue des Americas where I used my rudimentary French to order. Bad idea. We ended up with a plate of cooked Brussels sprouts—little cabbages. It only took moments to agree we were not really hungry.

A few hours later we boarded another train—maybe the Orient Express--and went to Ulm on the Danube (Ulm/Do) in Bavaria, a town that was already eleven hundred years old and had survived World War II. An Army staff car met us at the depot to take us the rest of the way to my new home in the old part of the city close to the place where Hitler's soldiers had been quartered, at Zinglerstrasse #73. I didn't intend to be rude to our English speaking guide, but I was. That's when—too late I realized afterward—I first displayed symptoms of FMD, the disastrous Foot in Mouth Disorder.

"What caused that?" I asked, pointing toward a large crater in the middle of the street. "And why doesn't the train station have a roof? Whatever happened?"

Maybe a tornado? Everywhere I looked I saw piles of rubble and buildings without windows. The signs of destruction were evident, but I couldn't recall reading about a bad storm hitting Germany. I was trying to be politely interested, but I should have kept quiet and not displayed my boundless ignorance.

"Just bomb holes," he said peering nonchalantly through spectacles now perched on his nose. He watched me closely.

I covered my gaping mouth with a white gloved hand. *Did he mean from the war?* Surely not! But I knew he did.

"Bombs?"

"Ja! Your Flyboys and the Brits dropped bombs every day at noon and midnight, week after week. That's all, leftover bomb holes. By the grace of God we carried on with our daily lives. We ate dinner at noon like usual with bombs bursting all around us. Some ran into shelters and the shelter took a direct hit. Others died on the street. I decided eating was important, so I ate. I slept through most of the midnight soirees. My people are dead bcause of Hitler, that crazy wallpaper hanger! We need more time to fix everything. We'll get around to it in a few years."

A few years! When the war ended in 1945 I was twelve. I'm twenty! That's eight years. I thought of another of Mister Poly's history lessons.He told us Rome wasn't built in a day. Of course, I did understand. It does take longer when you have to do it without modern machinery. Reconstruction was slow in Ulm because it had to be done with hand tools. But eight years? I couldn't imagine it taking that long in the United States.

"You speak English very well," I said attempting to retrieve my dignity. "Are you German?"

I didn't know what a German looked like. He said he wasn't and was born in Warsaw but lived in Ulm because sometimes, like today, he worked for Americans.

Bill had totally quit interacting—except professionally--with all foreign nationals, but after my humbling moment I warned him to be careful what he said to anybody and to think before speaking to avoid FMD.

Military wives and children are referred to as dependents, collaterals, or worse. I didn't like the word dependent but soon heard more offensive terms. Camp follower was more reprehensible and conjured up images of frontier whores chasing blue uniformed Union soldiers and prairie schooners. I was no whore! My grandmother taught me to be a lady. I was, and I am, and my actions prove it.

I was rankled that I was advised to avoid socializing with wives whose husbands outranked mine, and in fact, that such relation-ships were forbidden! I also learned class social division rested upon the shoulders of officers, who unlike Bill, had wives who were, unlike me, automatically considered to be ladies.

Sergeant Katz' wife said, "In shoyn! (End of the world!) Makes me? What? Chopped liver?" She counted to ten and smiled. "So? They're prejudiced? What's new?"

While residing in occupied Germany our government prohibited me from seeking gainful employment because they claimed German women *needed* to have jobs, but I didn't. Like it or not, I was dependent upon Bill for as long as we lived in Bavaria.

I began to explore our surroundings. My initial encounter with DPs (Displaced Persons), or refugees—intellectually challenging and emotionally charged as that was—left me feeling sad. Some Americans referred to DPs as "dregs of society." I called them half-alive, half-dead souls who didn't perish in a gas chamber, weren't shot in their own homes like Nantchi's sister, and didn't die from bomb blasts, disease or starvation. DPs had survived Hell and been chosen by God to survive and live, that's what I believed.

Survivors arrived in the American Zone in droves. Troops in Ulm warehoused them behind barbed wire close to the *kaserne* (barracks) near our apartment. Most suffered from grief and malnutrition. Now, eight years after the war ended, they were still there living in a zoo of homeless men, women, and children divided by age, nationality, religion, education, cultural diversity, or language, but united in misery.

The memory of those sunken cheeks people haunts me. I saw wistful eyes follow me when I walked to the store, and I watched skinny upturned hands poking through the wire fencing and felt those eyes beseech me for help. What could I do? I didn't know what to do. I did nothing and averted my eyes. I should have at least prayed. I could have done that, but I didn't. I told Bill they made me feel like a phony Christian.

"Fraternization is not permitted," he said. "Stay away or ignore them."

Most Germans, both urban and rural, and especially where we lived in Bavaria, had expected Germany to win the war. Though lacking amenities found in the erudite capital city of Berlin, the Danube River region of Bavaria became a popular Nazi stronghold. I wanted to hear firsthand accounts from people who blindly followed Hitler's road to perdition. Strangely, I didn't find a single person who knew anything at all about anyone being a Nazi.

I did meet survivors who complained about the scarcity of food, clothing, housing, and The Soviet Union. And more than a few said they traveled long distances to be helped by the "generous Americans" instead of the French. Nantchi was the one who touched my heart strings with insightful stories detailing how her capturers hurt her body but couldn't shake her Catholic faith, and she told stories about Russian peasant women who smuggled half a potato or other food to her and kept her from starving.

Following the end of World War II Russia strenuously objected to the Allied proposal of a four-way division of Germany that includ-ed restrictions denying Russia from seeking revenge on German civilians. Russia continued to pout. I asked Nantchi if they would dare invade Bavaria. I couldn't imagine it happening, but understood that she feared it.

"Would they dare? Ja! For sure! One day they will. Watch out for them!" she said.

I knew Russian communists despised rich people, royalty, and gypsies. Nantchi's father was a wealthy Transylvanian. He had gold, houses, and servants. Invading Russian soldiers shot her sister and mother, declared her father an enemy of the people sending him to die in a Siberian gulag, and enslaved Nantchi in Russia as a political prisoner.

I had trouble understanding. Back in Lawrence Park three Russian men passed our house going to and from work every day and didn't act or look dangerous. I was confused and had to admit that I knew little about Russia.

"Russian soldiers *will* come," Nantchi said. "When the war ended they give to me men's clothes and say walk to Germany, not go home. Those thieves stole our land. I'm sure they will round up and kill former prisoners, like me. Before they do, I'll take my baby and walk in the Danube River until we both drown. I will never be taken again by those filthy pigs!"

Nantchi looked upset so I changed the topic to talk about her infant son, Roland. Maybe that was a safe subject that wouldn't remind her of the past.

There were numerous grief stories and I listened to many but I couldn't empathize with everybody. Nantchi was unique. She was my friend, my role model, and my mentor. She made my heart weep and changed my perspectives about war, death, Russians, slave camps, survival, and more. In spite of suffering horrific hardships my new friend had an admirable, unwavering faith in God and was blessed with a happy spirit.

There are millions of people with stories similar to Nantchi's. War does that to populations. With exception of The Civil War American civilians have been fortunate with only a few first hand stories to tell until the World Trade Center was hit, The Fort Hood terrorist attack (incorrectly identified as work place violence), Oklahoma's tragedy, and the Chattanooga Recruit Center terrorist killing, etc. But none of that had occurred before I met Nantchi—a brave young woman only five years my senior.

Because of Nantchi's friendship I finally understood a little bit about the real world. I no longer was a young American on a holiday in Europe; I was part of a military command overseas. I began to guard my words and green State Department passport more carefully, read about Stalin and Mother Russia, gave up childish ways, and developed a mature interest in world events. I asked Bill what else I should do.

"We're sitting on a powder keg, Babe. We could be at war any moment. Russia remains a threat and we live in an occupied country. So adapt, Babe. Adapt."

How comforting! How helpful. Didn't he see I was doing that already?

Bill usually wore olive green fatigues, combat boots and a steel helmet. It was winter and there was no central heat at Zinglerstrasse #73. I wore jeans over jeans, sweaters over sweaters, socks over socks, and fur-lined boots I bought downtown. Sometimes I cocooned myself in Bill's lined Army field jacket, but even on sunny days my teeth chattered. When he was home, Bill made our room feel almost tolerably warm for several hours by building a fire in a small coal burning stove.

Hausfraus who didn't have an oven in their kitchen—like we didn't—stirred up a cake with eggs, milk, flour and sugar then carried it to the local bakery where the baker put it in his oven and for a few pennies baked it. I was a bit reluctant and didn't speak German fluently, but I decided to try doing it. I took a lemon meringues pie to the baker but he didn't understand when I instructed him with my limited vocabulary.

"Bake it no more than five minutes," I said. Or, thought I did.

Such a disaster! He baked it an hour.

Construction of government quarters would be completed soon and I knew our apartment would include central heat, refrigerators and ranges with ovens. I decided against more baking until we moved to Ford Barracks at the end of the trolley tracks miles from Zinglerstrasse #73.

CHAPTER 12

— ✃ —

Swedish Feet

ONE AFTERNOON I wore a new outfit purchased on the economy and Bill took me downtown to practice my language skills. My outfit and charade fooled everyone into believing I was a fraulein. Good for me? No. Not that day.

Bill dropped me off in front of the shoe store and went to park the car a block away. An old man approached me outside the store and asked for directions to some place I didn't know. He didn't understand, or didn't believe me when I explained in German that I was American, new in the city, and didn't know. An altercation followed.

"Sorry, I don't know," I said once in English and again in German while backing toward the shoe store. He was quite angry and aggressive.

He shook his skinny old finger in my face as a crowd gathered. He yelled words I didn't understand, and those I did. He said I was only pretending to be American, a disgrace to my heritage, and probably some GI's paid schatzie (sweetie). He spat on the ground to show his disgust. It occurred to me that maybe I had finally met a former Nazi, but I wasn't going to ask him any questions about it!

My Romanian accent and use of local idioms from talking with Nantchi had fooled him and he was convinced I was German, a whore, and a liar. Anxious to avoid more trouble if Bill arrived in uniform and caused a bigger scene, I needed to extricate myself.

In the nick of time I managed to escape inside the shoe store intending to forget about the prejudice of an old man still raving outside on the sidewalk. A smiling clerk welcomed me and declared she didn't speak English. *Yeah, right! Ha, ha!*

"Honestly, I'm not German. I am from Pennsylvania. The United States of America! My dress, this outfit—Kleidung?—came from Merkur's, that's true. Most of the time I wear American blue jeans. Ja? I'm American, not German! "

"Nicht," she said in the local vernacular, shaking her head and rolling her eyes heavenward. The girl was young. I believed she knew how to speak English.

"Ja! Americanishe. I'm American. And I bet you speak perfect English."

How do I convince a shoe clerk I'm not German? I quit trying and sat down. I suspected she understood at least some English; it was a required subject in German schools.

At a formal American/German social I had been expected to converse during dinner with the tall, dark and handsome seated beside me who said he was Prussian and didn't speak English. I only spoke a little Bavarian Low German— not taught in schools-- not used in Berlin and wanted to speak English.

"Didn't you study English in school?" I said. He nodded while kissing my hand.

"Ja," he admitted. "I can say, 'the barn is red.'" I smiled at his joke and we spoke German, or as close to that as I could manage.

I quit reminiscing about waltzing with the sexy Prussian who whirled me around and around, faster and faster, until I felt faint and turned my attention back to the clerk.

"Speak English," I told her and removed my shoe so she could check the size.

My feet are short and wide. Buying shoes—except in the children's department--in The United States is difficult, but in Europe my size is readily available. I wanted clogs with wooden soles like those favored by the young shampoo girl who washed my thick, long hair at the salon.

"Size thirty-five and a half, please. Bring out some red clogs, okay?" I said speaking English on purpose.

A glance toward the street showed Bill lounging against the building with a Lucky Strike dangling from his lower lip. The crowd had dispersed, no doubt very quickly with the arrival of an American who was part of the occupation army and the old man was gone. There'd be no more negative comments about me as long as Bill was visible.

In pidgin English and using hands and facial expressions the clerk explained that American women have long, narrow feet. I laughed and again said I was an American. Short of displaying my passport how could I convince her? She'd heard and watched the scene with the old man in front of the store and I lacked enough vocabulary to win a dispute. Could we mime?

I pantomimed going north, far north, farther.... until finally I must have accidentally done something, and she got it. Whoopee! She had studied geography somewhere and understood my father's people came from Sweden. That fact explained the shape of my feet to her satisfaction. She decided it was true, I was an American who could speak some German. Everything had changed. We were practically old friends or even kissing cousins because I had Swedish feet and Swedes have feet like Germans. That was news, but good news—at least for me!

"Okay," I said, relieved. "Let's find some red clogs. Bitte, bitte?" (pretty please)

I selected two pair. We parted with the colloquial expression meaning God is good, farewell, see you later, etc.as we vigorously pumped right hands in the local tradition.

Based on the reaction of the old man who scared me, I intended to speak nothing but English the rest of the day, but Bill said he was proud of me for learning to speak German so well that I fooled everyone.

"Right now, Babe, I'm starving. Let's find a restaurant, 'schatzie.' You do all the talking. Okay, Babe?"

I didn't really speak that well, but thousands of people who weren't natives were living there and they fractured it, too. If getting graded that day I earned an A in language arts and an F in fostering friendly relations between the German population and us *Ah-mees* (Americans).

We drove to the Gasthaus (beer hall) on the corner of Zinglerstrasse and each of us ordered Kalbfleisch und Kartoffeln— breaded veal cutlet with potatoes.

CHAPTER 13

— ✧ —

Tea Party Time

A FEW DAYS later Bill arrived home earlier than expected. When I heard his jeep screech to a stop outside the window and his combat boots on the stairs minutes later, I wondered what was happening.

"You'll be okay alone here a few days, right?" He didn't wait for an answer. "I'm off to Bordeaux, southwest of Paris, France."

I slipped from his embrace.

He grabbed his waterproof poncho and headed toward the door.

We're moving again? "Why?"

"Medical battalion's responsible for civilians. Just being prepared. We're mapping a dependent escape route."

Oh. How jolly! We have an escape route.

"Stop. Wait a minute. Escape? From what?"

"The Ruskies again. I mean the communists. The Russians. Kiss me, I gotta go."

There is no way to prepare to be married to a soldier. If you can't adapt, don't marry one. I agreed I'd be fine for a few days. He wouldn't have changed his plans if I'd said the opposite.

Will Rogers, the humorist said, "Even if you're on the right track, you'll get run over if you just sit there." I didn't intend to sit still and get run over while my husband was in France. When Anna invited me to join her and others at a tea party I gladly accepted.

Prior to 1939 Anna's family had owned the entire building we lived in. While Bill was gone I spent pleasant hours listening to her tell stories of growing up in Ulm, about her 1939 visit to New Jersey, her fondness for Jello, and how long, long ago she had met and married Karl.

One afternoon I cajoled Nantchi into telling spellbinding tales about her pre-war life as an heiress. That day a group of us had enjoyed fresh fruit covered flan topped with fresh whipped cream. I wondered about the pot of strong coffee we drank as five of us sat around a large round antique table in Anna's one room apartment.

German nationals like Anna couldn't afford to accept coffee even as a gift because the duty was too high. It was also scarce and remained expensive. I was pleasantly surprised it wasn't ersatz coffee. In fact, it was good. I usually preferred perked coffee but had become used to the instant Nescafe Bill bought in the PX. Anna's coffee tasted so good that afternoon that when Helene offered to pour more into my nearly empty cup I nodded.

Anna's daughter, Helene, and unemployed son-in-law, Adolf, entertained us with funny stories about their expanding parakeet business located in the screened porch off the kitchen. I said those pesky birds had provided several harrowing experiences for me when they flew around while I cooked.

"Vell, they need some exercise," Adolf said.

I told them about the day I had forgotten to put the lid back on our Nescafe and returned to the kitchen.

"I saw parakeets flying everywhere, but Adolf wasn't present. My open jar of Nescafe coffee was knee deep in parakeet poop, so I trashed it in the bin."

While re-filling my cup Helene said she had seen me do that. "From bin I took, to my mother I'm giving."

A very long pause followed. I held my cup half way to my lips. The only sound was the ticking of the mantel clock. I had a decision to make. I chose to laugh about it.

"I hope," I said smiling broadly, "that Nescafe coffee ala parakeet poop is nonlethal."

With that I tipped the antique porcelain cup to my lips and emptied it. The buzz of people talking returned, everyone laughed, and like a good will ambassador I gagged, and swallowed.

CHAPTER 14

─── ❧ ───

Made in Germany

BEFORE WORLD WAR II the entire second floor housed Anna's family only. Now, their apartment was partitioned into spaces for three generations of Anna's family, Nantchi's family, a big dog named Ano, Bill and me.

We had the corner room above a grocery, across from a bakery. One window looked down at a tree and a busy tavern by a trolley stop. Everyone at Zinglerstrasse #73 shared one tiny closet with a pull chain commode, a communal bathing room, and cold kitchen with a cement floor, without running hot water, refrigeration, oven, or utensils.

Nantchi would have paid less money for the same space but Bill willingly paid eighty marks--equal to twenty American dollars--rent because housing was at a premium due to bombed out or razed buildings and an influx of civilian military dependents, like me, who complicated the situation. Our space was cramped and lacked privacy, but this is where we lived April 9th, 1954 when young Hildie gave birth in Ulm at Frauen Klinik and told the American Army chaplain she wanted to give up her child so he'd have a chance at a life she couldn't provide.

I didn't know that chaplain, but I did know there were thousands of deserted, adoptable babies neither German families nor over-crowded orphanages wanted. Bi-racial, black and white innocents faced starvation and death unless they were rescued. Adoption became popular with Americans and institutions rushed to foster German-American adoptions.

My doctors in Erie had said I could conceive again, but couldn't physically carry a baby full term. Bill and I wanted a child. Orphanages were full. It was simple math. We decided to adopt. Bill filled out the required paperwork for visas, etc.—probably in triplicate on a typewriter, and submitted it to the proper authorities. We started waiting. Army people are experienced at waiting. Only a few days passed before the chaplain contacted me to say a baby boy was ready for adoption at the Women's Clinic downtown in Ulm not far from the famous Munster, the huge church near city hall in the center of town.

"He was born April 9th. Both mother and child are healthy. Father is gone. She'll give him up because she can't work and he'd starve. She's Catholic but doesn't care if he isn't. She also said his parents should give him a name. She looks a lot like you, Mrs. Gill. Interested?"

"We want a baby, but Sergeant Gill requested a girl. I'll go ask him if a boy is okay."

When I asked Bill he said I should go get the baby but he couldn't leave the dental clinic or drive me to town. I was surprised. That should have been a clue, but I was too young and new to Army life to recognize it. Bill was used to making decisions for others having less rank and they carried them out. Apparently, he lumped me in the same category. They obeyed, why not me? Much later I realized I should have waited until Bill could go with me.

I rode the Army shuttle bus back off post, caught a trolley, and went downtown to see the infant and make arrangements. He looked perfect. Doctor Vogel (bird) told me he was three days old and ready to go. The clinic didn't offer any instructions, advice, or help and handed an eight pound swaddled infant to me without comment.

In spite of tons of Marshall Plan food shipped via my former employer, The Mutual Security Administration, Germany had too many postwar mouths to feed. As more mothers were abandoned by American GIs German social service civilians tried to assume the overwhelming chore of caring for German-American children left behind. It wasn't part of a master plan to destroy Hitler's pure Aryan race by mongrelizing the population, but it worked like it was. Rampant, out of control, cross-breeding flourished causing a genealogical nightmare but some sticklers still cling to the idea they are 100 percent German. Due to relocations of people from around the globe, and the ensuing baby boom, I doubt that could be possible for people born after the war.

We named our blue-eyed, blonde son William Mark, but called him Marcus, or Mark, to avoid future confusion since Bill's name was William. A year before it was time to return to Pennsylvania, and much to the surprise of everyone, I delivered a healthy child at the American hospital in Stuttgart March 25, 1955 proving the Pennsylvania gynecologists were mistaken. We named our son for two Biblical heroes and christened him Michael David.

German authorities sent a social worker to our house to ask if we wanted to return Mark. I was shocked by what the social worker said.

"We need to be sure you want to keep him. Since now you got one of your own?"

Grandmother Hattie-Becky Leonard would have considered adoption a no-no. She, like many others, believed in the secret Know-Nothing party of the 1840s. Asked to explain reasons for limiting immigration they usually refused to answer, or shrugged and said, "I know nothing" earning the nick-name of The Know-Nothings. Now I suspected my Grandmother Leonard of trying from the grave to convince me to send Mark back.

Grandmother had never accepted my father because his family had come too recently from Sweden and she considered him and his relatives, and everyone who hadn't lived in the United States before her cut-off date of 1832, interlopers and unwelcome Johnny Come Lately (s). My maternal grandmother loved me, but she was a snob with a capital S and she loathed the idea of adoption.

Adoption wasn't a new idea, but a lot of our relatives refused to accept it. After we arrived in Pennsylvania we encountered opposition from several older family members, although to their credit they tried to hide it, but it didn't deter our decision to love Mark as our child.

I wondered what the social worker thought of my answer. I believe I shocked her, but she had shocked me first with her attitude and then with her question about returning Mark. I still remember her exact words.

"Vee have to take babies back all the time. You give him back und vee find some other family. Ja? Up to you, Frau Gill."

"You take babies back? But they're people! How bizarre!"

"Vell, you know? Sometimes they just don't fit."

Like a suit of clothes that doesn't fit?

"No! Never! How dare you!"

"Ja? Vell, I had to ask." She made a notation in her notebook, closed it, and stood up. I was sure there would be no more visits from German authorities.

"You can go to Munich," she said, "and get Marcus a visa and passport. Good luck, Frau Gill. I'm closing the case file today."

As far as the authorities were concerned, Mark was our child now and no longer any of their concern. She extended her hand to shake mine, left our apartment, and disappeared from our lives, but not from my memory.

We took Mark to a passport photographer and Bill drove to Munich to apply for his passport and visa. Mark would travel with a German passport when we went to The States, but Michael had to share my passport because he was a minor but considered an American by birth and too young to need his own.

We were told both boys would enjoy dual citizenship until they grew up and then they would have to choose. An official some-where in Ulm warned me to be sure the boys remembered that they had to choose American before the cut off year or be drafted into the German army. I think the age of declaration was twenty-five, but it didn't matter because Michael joined the U.S. Army when he was eighteen losing his German citizenship and Mark became a nat-uralized American citizen in Columbia, South Carolina at age five.

CHAPTER 15

——— ❧ ———

The Travelers

ON MARK'S SECOND birthday, April ninth, we moved out of government quarters and hurried by night train to the coastal city of Bremerhaven where we waited three days for the MSTS Patch. It was much smaller and had fewer accommodations than the USS United States I had sailed on three years before. We slept in narrow steel bunks suspended from the walls, but it got us home.

On the third day at sea we heard the ship's engines grind to a stop. Sponsors and dependents were ordered below deck and told to stay there. Somebody didn't want us to observe something. Bill met a sailor who confided they planned to practice dropping depth charges. Apprehensive passengers waited as the crew blew up something in the middle of the Atlantic Ocean—or, whatever they really did. Soon, familiar chimes sounded bong-itty, bong, bong announcing it was chow time and the end of another routine day in the life of a military family.

Five days later Mark was seasick all over a sergeant wearing his Class A's for debarking. I was horrified, but the sergeant was nice about it. I took Mark to our cabin to clean up leaving Bill alone to apologize and continue feeding Baby Michael. Mike ate more than Mark—always a fussy eater and colicky--and at thirteen months weighed thirty-two pounds.

The next day the boys and I were topside watching our slow approach to the Statue of Liberty. As I gawked at the New York City skyline I didn't notice a Health Department boat pull alongside and people boarding the Patch. Suddenly, I was ordered to go wait in our cabin to be inspected.

What? Inspected! Are we immigrants?

We three obedient dependents went to our cabin and waited. I can't remember where Bill was. Maybe he was helping with the inspection. It was a classic example of hurry up and wait that lasted a couple of hours. Cooped up with fussy little ones it felt like we waited for days.

Sailors removed our luggage and promised it would be waiting on the dock. I have no idea where it went, or if Customs was involved. I hoped to find it soon; the children needed clothes and I was anxious to get to the airport for the next leg of our journey. But once berthed we weren't allowed to debark. I bounced Michael on my left hip wishing he would learn to walk. With one hand I also maintained a death grip on Mark's wrist so he wouldn't run off—which given a chance, he would. Finally, we were directed to a gangplank leading to the pier.

We stood on the pier in long horizontal lines shrouded in damp mist and shivering in a chilly wind whipping off the Atlantic. As dusk fell I asked Bill what we were waiting for and reminded him we had a plane to catch.

"The Army likes to wait," he said.

"Waiting? Standing here? Freezing with two lively children playing tug of war?"

We waited. And, we waited. Surrounded by military uniforms we waited some more. My aching 100 percent civilian muscles began to scream bloody murder and threatened to give up. This was certainly a strange way to end a sea voyage and I was getting madder and madder. I don't like complainers, but this was ridiculous. I told the boys we were playing a game called Whisper and they had to remain perfectly still and quiet while Daddy and I whispered.

"William," I hissed. "I'm freezing and the boys are wet and cold. Why aren't we going? Can't you do something?"

"Be patient, Babe. I can't do anything about this right now."

"I have been patient! What are we waiting for? What's happening?"

"A briefing. I have to stand it. I can't leave before hearing some jackass give us a welcome home speech, and you have to stand right beside me. Don't talk."

At last I saw a pimpled second lieutenant. He cleared his throat and began the briefing, or whatever it was. I listened intently hoping to learn something of value. What I did hear was a satirical rant degrading to me and our returning troops including noncom master sergeants, like Bill. We endured trash talk that made me furious and it wasn't even directed my way. It was gutter rudeness amplified. My face felt as hot and red as Rudolph's nose —I was insulted and angry!

He tried humor; it wasn't funny. Do returning soldiers really need to be told to wear pajamas at their mother's house? Or, be advised not to solicit sex from American girls by offering nylons or chocolate bars? "First," he advised, "say hello and compliment her looks. Then ask, how much?"

I mentally stuck my fingers in my ears as the welcome home (a misnomer to end all misnomers) dragged on. My new high heel pumps pinched and hurt, my nerves were shot, and by the time he finished I was very cold and damp.

"The kids need dry clothes. So do I. Where's our luggage? Do something!"

Bill had no idea where our luggage was but he guessed it was sent on to Erie. "No time to change now. We've got to run for it or miss our flight to Erie. We can't stay here. A hotel is too expensive. You can change them in Pennsylvania. Let's boogie."

"You aren't serious?"

I could see he was. His temple nerve pulsated, and that was a clear danger signal. We managed to phone ahead to the airport to let them know we were on the way. Using his most assertive voice Bill barked orders into the phone.

"We're coming! Hold that plane!"

Aside to me he said, "We've got to catch that flight. Hubba, hubba, honey. Move it! Move it!"

I don't know how we got there in time but the plane was still warming up on the runway with both propellers spinning. When Bill saw that he ordered me to carry the boys and run. *I* can't *do that. Can I*? Wait *a darn minute*!

It meant carrying sixty-five pounds of squirming kids while running in the dark across the tarmac wearing three inch heels without breaking an ankle, falling down, or dropping a kid. Before I could protest he left me standing there while he, like the quarterback in a championship play-off, sprinted down the field toward the goal line carrying five heavy leather suitcases and his duffle bag and hollering, "Hold that plane!"

My already exhausted, wet and cold body shuddered at the notion of carrying both children, but with a boy under each arm, my shoulder strap purse slapping a tattoo across my back, and our camera case bouncing across my breast with each step, I ran toward the light from the open door of the airplane. *Did I sign up for this? Is it grounds for divorce*?

Once aboard I saw we were the only passengers on a red-eye flight from New York City to Erie International Airport where my parents were staying up way past their bed time to wait for us.

A few days later Bill left Erie to report in for his new assignment at Walter Reed Army Medical Center (WRAMC) in Washington, D.C.

The plan was for me to stay in Erie until he found an apartment and our household goods arrived from Germany. I was happy to stay longer in Erie so I could see Pati's new baby and help my mother celebrate her fifty-third birthday.

Everything changed the day Bill's father arrived intending to whisk us away like Superman saving Lois Lane from a burning building. In less than twenty hours Bob and Grace Gill drove from Statesville to Erie, found my parents' house, and were chomping at the bit to turn around the same day and drive right back to North Carolina taking the boys and me with them.

"You're kidding," I said.

Didn't my father-in-law ever sleep?

"I've waited too long to see my grandbaby. Y'all air coming home with me now, heah? Billy can come get you there when it's time."

He expected me and the boys to Hi-ho Silver it to Statesville. I tried to resist, but that didn't work. He was persuasive. My parents didn't say anything to try to stop us.

A genius must have packed for us in Ulm because in spite of climate changes from cold to very hot we had everything we needed. I don't know how Bill fared. I never packed his clothes. He rolled and stuffed his own things into a duffle bag which he always personally carried.

Bill phoned with news that he had found an apartment. I told relatives in Statesville and invited them to visit us in Washington. After supper the same evening we boarded a Southern Rail sleeper. I hoped we would arrive in D.C. rested but two oversugared, hyped up toddlers fought all the way to Virginia no matter what I did. It was terrible. Nobody got any sleep creating a sullen and grouchy trio when Bill met us.

Our new home was a first floor apartment in a red brick building in a prominently Jewish community in Langley Park within easy walking distance to The University of Maryland. It seemed great

78

until Bill confessed our household goods didn't arrive and were actually lost. We had an empty apartment.

"I'm sure they'll find our stuff soon, Babe. Don't worry."

"We've been vagabonds for months. You say don't worry? Ha! Let's go to a hotel."

"Do you have cash for a hotel?"

"You don't?"

I staggered from lack of sleep and was hopeful this nightmare would end.

"Nope. Put it all on the apartment rent and security deposit. I'll have more soon. Missed you and the boys. Give me a kiss, Babe."

"No more kissing until you answer me. What do we do?"

"We bivouac. Sleep on the floor. Thursday is payday. Come the week-end we'll go get our stuff you've got stored in your dad's attic. Don't we have a sofa bed up there? We'll rent a U-Haul-It and bring back everything you left up north. Piece of cake. But tonight? We're camping out."

The boys fell asleep on the hardwood living room floor wrapped in blankets Bill brought with him. One of them started crying. I tried to fake sleep. When that didn't work I said, "I hear somebody crying for his daddy." He took care of it without complaint. When everything was quiet again I felt Bill wrap his strong arms around me. It was good to be home.

We left Thursday night after supper and by midnight were speeding through the mountains of West Virginia and Pennsylvania while both boys slept soundly. To pass the time I sang hillbilly songs until Bill begged me to stop. Then we argued about the pronunciation of a mountain range. Bill insisted it was Appa-latch-in because students from Appalachian College near Statesville said it was. I was just as sure it was Appa-lay-chee-in, an Iroquois Indian word. Following an hour long debate we decided on a compromise. North of Pittsburgh we'd say it my way.

Driving past sleeping little towns on route seventy-nine had been fun on the way north, but the ride back dragging a loaded trailer behind our Chevy coupe was not. It was July and breathlessly hot even at night. And we were tired from working all afternoon carrying things from the attic and packing them in the trailer.

It had taken several hours and without help from my former classmate, Herbie, we would have had to leave the sofa behind because I couldn't help lift it. As soon as the trailer was full Bill said he intended to drive it right back to Maryland. Daddy didn't like that idea but when he saw Bill was determined, he fixed sandwiches and a thermos of coffee for us and we left Erie about three o'clock the same day we got there, but didn't go far. A few hours later traffic came to a standstill.

We all were hungry, hot, and tired. I began unwrapping ham sandwiches and hoped the cars ahead would move forward before Bill grew more impatient. I was sorry for him and knew he felt miserable because of a large number of—more than a dozen—carbuncles in varying stages, and also from frustration and exhaustion, and I knew he hated sitting in stalled traffic.

The famous evangelist, Oral Roberts, never knew about it but because of him we were forced to stay overnight in a motel/hotel/ tourist cabin that should have been condemned! I have to admit the idea of staying in a cute little cabin had been mine.

"Let's stop for the night," I said as we sat in the long line of bumper-to-bumper traffic not moving at all. The narrow road didn't allow us to pass to the head of the line and Bill hated playing follow the leader. I joked that walking to D.C. might have been faster. Bill didn't laugh.

"Must be an accident or license check ahead," Bill said. "I'll find a back road detour. Oh, shit. It's some kind of revival. Looks like cops are detouring everybody. What next?"

Police directed traffic around anyone trying to turn left to the Oral Roberts revival tent. Bill saw a flashing sign advertising cabins and pulled in the driveway. We got out and locked the doors. The cabins were old, in need of paint, and uninviting. Inside looked worse than outside and I dreaded seeing it in daylight—a faux iron bed, no radio, phone, hot water, tub or shower.

"How do I wash up?"

I wish I hadn't asked. Bill said In Korea he shaved and bathed in his helmet. He told me to take a whore's bath in the sink. While an outside neon sign flashed on and off like a migraine headache I looked at the sink, turned away, and crawled into the bed and tried to feign sleep with the boys between us on a lumpy, plastic covered mattress that made a crinkle noise if anyone stirred. I was so tired I began laughing hysterically. Bill kissed me and advised I get some shut-eye or at least be quiet so he could.

I said, "Ha!"

"We won't stay all night. I just need to catch a few winks."

Bill fell asleep, but I lay awake wondering what might be under the bed. What if there were bedbugs? I worried about the safety of our things in the parking lot. Was the tarp securely closed over our furniture in the U-Haul? I planned a grocery list so we could stop at a Piggly Wiggly before going home and I spent several minutes pondering whether or not I needed a haircut. I discarded the idea of removing any clothing and waited for dawn.

Bill had no idea—and couldn't have understood. He had told me often enough that he wasn't afraid of anything and I believed him, but I was different. I was afraid of lots of things and in the Happy Home rustic cabin in the woods surrounded by bugs, bears, snakes, wolves, and who knew what else, I was afraid to close my eyes. I sat propped up in bed in the semi-dark wishing to be home—not in a filthy tourist cabin forcing myself not to cry.

Something, I have no idea what it was, but something caused me to think about Germany and March twenty-eighth of the previous year and to remember every detail of the day we brought Michael home from Stuttgart. I held back tears until the coppery taste of blood alerted me and I realized I had bitten a chunk out of the inside of my lip. Then a feeling of sadness and loneliness took over and memories flooded in as hot tears cascaded down my cheeks and I relived *that* day.

CHAPTER 16

———— ❦ ————

Duty is a Four Letter Word

IT WASN'T REALLY such a terrible thing that happened, but I was furious after Bill told me about a pending court-martil he felt duty bound to attend. I felt sucker-punched when Bill announced he had to deposit three-day-old Michael and me on the sidewalk without helping us inside. Stunned, and weak from childbirth, I watched his taillights disappear around the corner. The street was deserted, just like I felt. I looked into the face of my new baby and knew I couldn't remain there in the noontime heat feeling sorry for myself. I slowly put one foot in front of the other.

Memories of that day were bitter déjà vu. Disappointment laced with residual anger filled my head until images behind my eyes hurt. I willed them to stop but once begun they didn't stop and I was forced to recall every minute, of every hour, of that entire day, beginning with telling a nursing sister good-bye. She wore robes like a nun but said she was a Lutheran Sister. Whatever she was, she is the one who accompanied our new baby and me from the maternity section, to the exit of the converted German hotel in Stuttgart, and waited outside with us until Bill arrived in our car.

At the end of the war The United States had requisitioned that hotel and declared it a hospital for Americans--making it temporarily part of the United States (like embassy grounds)--where our son, Michael, was born au naturel slightly more than seventy-two hours earlier and because Bill and I were Americans, and he was

83

born on "American soil" the State Department granted him citizenship of the United States, and gave him a document from The State Department to prove it. Because he was born in Germany he would also have dual citizenship.

Bill opened the car door and I slid in holding the baby securely in my arms. During the hour ride from Stuttgart to Ulm Bill didn't mention anything about a court-martial. All of a sudden at the last moment when we were in front of our apartment he told me he had urgent business at headquarters and it was his duty to be there.

"Today? You're not serious!"

"No fooling, Babe. I wish I didn't have to go, but I do. This is life or death stuff."

I did understand it was serious. Bringing home a baby was, too. I hated to hear what else he was saying. I also hated remembering that it was an Army wife's duty to help her husband perform his duty by not whining or causing any trouble of any kind. I didn't have to like it. I just had to do it. It was my duty now to help him.

The court-martial was being held because somebody suspected one of the sergeants of homosexual activity that--if proved—would make him unsuitable for duty. He'd face his accusers and have an opportunity to defend himself, but it was well known that he was guilty. An ad hoc committee of military personnel would convene to make a judgment that would probably result in a general dis-charge, in which case he might keep some of his benefits. But the outcome of the trial, no matter what they decided, would certainly end the sergeant's long exemplary military career.

Everyone knew Bill went by the book. The sergeant knew he wouldn't get special treatment just because he had been friends with Bill and they both knew there would be consequences includ-ing the possibility of a dishonorable discharge, or even prison.

Bill was aware of the homophobic opinions held by the majority of his men, and that in the 1950s homosexuals were unwelcome in the Army, and historically such behavior had been dealt with harshly since the first one was drummed out of the corps in 1778.

Everyone also knew that it was every soldier's duty to report such activity up the chain of command and that it was a court–martial offense. Apparently somebody had followed orders, done his duty, and reported such a suspicion.

I didn't object to the court-martial per se. The sergeant had been discreet but he knew what he did was against regulations. Even I understood that going against rules and regulations was breaking a cardinal law and a big no-no. What I objected to was being surprised and unceremoniously deposited onto the sidewalk on a hot day in a foreign country with a brand-new baby forced to fend for myself when I was weakest.

It didn't matter what reason Bill had. At first, I thought he was teasing but when I realized he wasn't I was shocked, then livid. Now a year later I conjured up the way I'd felt that day and experienced the all consuming anger and sadness return. And I felt bad—not for the sergeant whose life was destroyed by a court-martial—I was too vain to worry about a stranger who had been kicked out of the Army for unbecoming conduct.

I felt bad because of the way Bill behaved. He should have treated me more fairly, he should have told me in advance so I could plan, but he hadn't and I was mad at him for that, and because he never apologized. He never had a clue how much he had hurt my feelings. That hurt, too.

Why would he apologize? He wouldn't. He didn't think he had done anything wrong. Bill was a loyal and excellent Regular Army soldier who followed orders, did his duty, and had no idea that he'd run over me with a tank.

I continued rationalizing what had happened a year ago. I still blamed Bill for deserting me when I needed him and I blamed him for the crumby motel/hotel, too. We could have stayed in Erie and slept in safety on clean sheets in my old room if he hadn't been in such an all-fire hurry to "hit the road."

After considering all these things and how they made me feel, did I really want to live this life and be an Army wife? I had to think about that. While I thought I replayed the memory of our trip home from the military hospital in Stuttgart.

๛

While Michael slept in my arms we chatted about this and that and hadn't been talking about anything in particular when I mentioned cars.

"I hear new cars in the States are two-tone. What do you think of that?"

"It won't catch on, Babe. I like this plain black British Ford, don't you?"

I told Bill I liked it fine but was curious to see what a two-tone car looked like.

"And what about red. Why haven't I seen a red one? Red's nice. Let's have a red car next time. Maybe get a two-tone, red and white?"

He dismissed my suggestion as impossible and said red was reserved for fire trucks and emergency vehicles as he tenderly kissed the top of the baby's head and then mine and said he loved us. Bill always drove with his right arm around my shoulders and that day as usual his left elbow hung out the window and he steered the car with the fingers of his left hand. As we skidded around a sharp curve he pulled me closer until our bodies were touching, but he didn't slow down even as we rode dangerously

86

close to the edge on the narrow road. I looked down but couldn't see all the way to the valley below.

"Hey! Hot rod! Keep your eyes on the road and both hands on the steering wheel. And slow down! Are you trying to kill us! Slow down!"

My words fell on deaf ears. We continued speeding down the mountain until I moved as far from him as I could get and hugged the door on my side of the car.

"Ah! Babe. Don't do that. Okay. I'll slow down some if you come back over here."

Hitler's Autobahn was built to quickly transport supplies and troops. Instead of taking that highway we traveled all the way home on back roads through some of the most beautiful country in the world and except for having to sit on a "Whoopee" pillow I enjoyed the ride. I also enjoyed seeing that the snow was gone and green had returned to the Alps. A few white spring flowers poked up to look around making the scene post card perfect.

"This reminds me of mountains near Pittsburgh."

"Looks a whole lot like Korea, Babe. Lots of mountains there."

I made a mental note to find out if Korea, Erie, and the Bavarian Alps were all on the thirty-eighth parallel and had four seasons like Pennsylvania.

"Are you going to go to work tomorrow?"

I expected him to say no, but he didn't.

"Yeah. And I've got the duty tomorrow night. I'm covering for Johnson. Sorry, Babe, but duty calls. You'll be okay, right?"

He didn't wait for an answer and I ignored his question.

"Duty? You have the duty? Overnight? CQ in the dental clinic? Baloney! You don't get the duty! What duty?"

"You know, Charge of Quarters. CQ. Yeah, I don't usually get it, but I traded for it."

An older, wiser Army wife once said, "Your husband isn't married to you, he's married to the Army. Duty will always come first." *Wasn't it his duty to take care of me?*

I wondered what he traded and why, but didn't ask. Like all units medics traded linens, alcohol, pills, surgical equipment, etc., for whatever they needed but couldn't requisition. It was so commonplace to swap items that I wasn't very curious, and it didn't matter. But that he would be gone tomorrow night, that did matter!

For several miles we rode without speaking. I started planning my afternoon.

Michael, poor baby, needed to be unswaddled. I peeled off one blanket at a time while sweat rolled down his nose and chin. I decided since Mark was at Alma's he could wait a while until Bill went to get him. I was hungry and anxious to learn about Bill's plans for lunch and hoped he had something waiting for us. I daydreamed about taking a nap and temporarily put Bill's CQ duty out of mind so I could think about how lucky we were to have a healthy new son. I must have been dozing about twelve forty-five when we pulled to a halt in front of our apartment building.

"We're home, Babe."

For some unknown reason Bill left the motor running. I didn't move to get out of the car and waited for him to come around and open the door, but he didn't.

"Can't come in with y'all, Babe. It's getting late and I've gotta be on time. Court-martial starts at thirteen hundred. My duty to be there, and not late. There's lunch stuff in the fridge. Later, alligator."

Why didn't you come for us after the court-martial? I can't climb those stairs by myself. What if I drop the baby? I'm in a foreign country thousands of miles from home. Don't go! I managed to open the door and step out before he pulled away.

He yelled out the window that he loved me as he sped from the Housing Area.

I was alternately angry, scared, feeling betrayed, deserted, and resolved. I stood on the sidewalk staring at an eighteen family gray cement block apartment building sans elevators, and knew it was up to me to climb the stairs to our apartment although I was feeling weak and doubted I could do it. The word duty rolled around on my tongue leaving a bad taste in my mouth.

Ours was a furnished second floor apartment. We had six rooms including a complete kitchen, running how water, a tub and shower, Rosenthal china, large picture windows, and all new furniture creating a huge improvement over our one room deal on Zinglerstrasse #73.

I knew I couldn't stay outside on the sidewalk forever. Holding onto the railing with one hand and cradling the baby with the other I finally managed to get to our apartment and drag myself inside to a yellow plush chair near the door where I collapsed. Gasping for breath I laid the baby tummy down across my lap and leaned back. I sat there like that with Michael on my lap wondering what to do next. The doorbell rang.

I reached the lever and opened the door hoping Bill had changed his mind and returned. It was Mark's babysitter, Alma, and Mark was with her.

"Soon's I seen y'all's car, I knowed you'd be awanting Mark. Bye, hon. Gotta run."

And like yesterday is gone for good so was she leaving me with a hungry, rambunctious toddler who looked like he'd grown in the past three days.

Mark wanted to see the new infant—a brother for our adopted first-born. I turned Michael so he could look. Mark pressed against my knees and peered into the baby's face. I hadn't been sure how he might react to another baby in the house and hoped he wouldn't be jealous. Fortunately, he seemed to be okay with it.

At least Mark was calm, usually he wasn't. That afternoon if he had started to jump out a window I couldn't have moved to stop him, that's how exhausted I felt. I watched as Mark outlined Michael's features with his chubby little finger before looking up at me with big blue eyes smiling.

I said, "baby" and Mark tried to copy me, but couldn't quite say it.

The doorbell rang again. Was Alma coming back to watch Mark and help me?

No. Wrong again. It was a man holding a long white floral box. "Wrong address," I said firmly closing the door in his face and sitting down again.

A few minutes passed before there was a persistent knock on the door. The same man stood before me holding out the box and insisted that I look at the name and address on it. I read: Mrs. Gill 2-B.

"Do I owe you money? I don't have any money."

"Nein. Weidershoen, Frau Gill."

I accepted the box from his hands and began to have nice thoughts about my husband who had sent flowers since he had to dump me like he did. I smiled as I carried Michael and the box to the dining room table with Mark toddling behind clutching the tail of my skirt. Twelve long stem roses nestled in the box with green tissue paper. A minute later my happy bubble burst. They weren't from Bill.

They were from my beloved Aunt Elda. I sat down with Michael in my arms and rocked back and forth keening. That set off a chain reaction. Mark screamed. Blame it on hormones, postpartum blues, homesickness or something else, but I overreacted. I thought about

Elda who was three thousand miles away in Chautauqua, New York. I loved my aunt more than ever.

And Bill? That duty bound rat who jumped ship? That dirty double-crossing deserter? Ha! I refused to think about First Sergeant Gill, the *extremely important* soldier who chose to sit on a court-martial instead of staying home with us! And I envisioned throwing poison darts at him.

Elda's flowers made me think about her and my mother, and about a poem titled *Rock* that was often recited by Ruth Leonard, and I hummed Rock of Ages, Rock-a-bye-Baby, and returned to the poem Ruth talked about and maybe wrote. I recited it sing-song style for the boys.

ROCK

I wish I was a little rock

a sitting on a hill

I wouldn't eat, I wouldn't sleep

I wouldn't even wash

I'd just sit still ten thousand years

and rest myself, by gosh!

That's how I felt last year and again this year wide awake in a wretched cabin watching car headlights slide across the ceiling at measured intervals while I recalled details of last March until I heard a police foghorn loudly ordering drivers to keep moving. Finally, there were no more headlights coming in the window and I had to be content with the motel's vacancy sign flashing on and off.

Before he fell asleep Bill said we would only stay long enough for him to catch a few winks. I wished him awake but when he stirred in his sleep he rolled over onto his side and didn't waken. I stared at his back. It was a disgusting field of infection. It looked painful and I felt remorse for thinking mean things about him. He must have been silently suffering all day. For lack of anything else to do I pondered the origin of our contagion and concocted a step-by-step method of eliminating it.

During my one year trial period in nurses' training at Hamot Hospital, I learned in a microbiology class that to rid ourselves of things like "staff" infections—in our case carbuncles—it became necessary to stringently isolate the patient and sterilize his clothes, towels, and bedding in an autoclave. I knew what to do to eradicate the infection. What I wanted to know was how we got it in the first place and how to prevent getting it again.

Propped against the headboard—it was that type bed—and concerned about getting infectious diseases from secret bed companions lurking in the mattress, my thoughts returned to Elda and the red roses she sent for the new baby then quickly reverted to the present time and carbuncles again. Focus, I told myself. Slow down and focus.

My high school art teacher, Miss Sack, often cautioned me to quit rushing. She was right. I needed patience. I told myself to remember that this too shall pass and recognize it is a phase. I tried to convince myself that one day carbuncles will be a thing we'll look back at and laugh. I was trying to be patient, but not very good at it.

For the fifth time in two minutes I looked at my gold Bulova graduation gift from Grandmother Leonard. I shook it and held it up to my ear to hear it ticking. Was it only two o'clock, a.m., zero two hundred hours Greenwich Mean Time in London and the United States Army? Only two o'clock! I might have to wait three or four more hours sitting up like this?

I tried mind over matter and told myself to go to sleep. It must have helped and I must have finally fallen asleep whispering "patience" like a mantra because when I opened my eyes Bill and the boys were dressed and sunshine streamed through the filthy window. With a start I remembered where I was. Bill's words from the night before echoed in my head. I saw the sink and thought about who might have washed there. I shuddered. I'd shower at home.

"Come on, Sleepyhead. I doubted you'd be able to sleep in this flea trap, but you slept like a log. Let's motor, Babe," he said snapping his fingers. "We'll grab a bite down the road. Right, kids?"

I jumped from the bed and announced I was ready. In the car I began thinking about carbuncles again. Bill was barely able to put his back against the seat cushion without wincing. I told him he needed medical attention and said I was sorry that he had so many sores. Then I made a confession.

"I was mad at you for the horrible hotel, but I'm over it."

"Good. Scootch over here, Babe and kiss me. If you snuggle up close as you can I'll forgive you for being mad at me."

I wondered how it got all reversed like that.

Bill worked at one of the most prestigious hospitals in the world. Surely he could see a doctor about his condition before the sores became infected or spread. But maybe he wouldn't be willing to do that. He didn't ever admit failure. He would see it as a failure if he had to go to a doctor.

Bill believed he was a perfect physical specimen and didn't have problems. But carbuncles affected all of us and we'd had them four months. Way too long. Something was letting staphylococci breed in our family. One of us had to seek medical help. If Bill refused I'd take Michael again.

The Army pediatrician in Germany had tried to convince me lack of sanitation was at fault. I was upset that day but clenched my fist in my pocket knowing the doctor was wrong. I didn't know what caused us to have carbuncles, but it wasn't from being dirty. Apparently he didn't know either. What I did know was that he was a captain and captain outranks sergeant so I shouldn't argue. I took Michael home with written instructions on how to keep him clean and I didn't take him back there.

Michael's sores had been the first and were confined to his scalp. I started thinking of him as little ground zero. Mark bore a couple of carbuncle scabs, but only a few scattered open sores. I had three or four including a big one located in a place I couldn't see. I was miserable waiting for it to ripen as it interfered with sitting or walking and eventually required a trip to the emergency room at WRAMC.

I was seen by a clerk, then an Army nurse and a white-coated doctor. They spoke to each other in muted tones while examining the large carbuncle I had complained about.

"This will hurt. Sorry," the doctor said as he lanced and drained the sore.

The Army nurse leaned forward to whisper in my ear.

"Most dependents shouldn't even be here, and I'd gladly trade places with them. But not with you, honey. Huh, uh. With you? You I wouldn't trade with for nothing."

That little conversation made me know I'd been right to seek medical attention in spite of Bill who thought he could take care of whatever ailed me. I had put my foot down and told him I needed a *real* medical person—not a medic, but when I insisted upon seeing a doctor he said he'd watch the boys and I could drive myself there.

Bill was proud of his straight picket fence, a term he used to describe his physical condition. It meant perfect and he was determined to keep it that way even to the point of denial. I had already observed all military personnel living around us looked very fit and healthy. It made sense for the soldiers, but dependents were also expected to be in perfect condition.

One day I overheard two soldiers talking about invalid spouses who needed to be shipped back to wherever they came from. Bill probably agreed with them. Like many others he believed people should "fake it until you make it" and if you don't enjoy perfect health and can't pretend you have it, bye, bye. ASAP.

I tried to stay in good condition, but a trip to the ER had plainly been indicated. While I was still at WRAMC I made an appointment for Michael for the next day and wrote on the form repeated infections of unknown origin as a reason. My mistake. That notation intrigued doctors who used it as a basis for a diagnosis of leukemia.

The pediatrician called in three other Army doctors to take a look. I guess I was supposed to be intimidated by such famous doctors taking an interest, but I distrusted them. One, who plainly had rank, took charge and began by leveling a battery of confusing questions but ignored my answers. Rank has its privileges (RHIP) so I bit my tongue and waited. He began writing on a piece of paper attached to a brown clipboard and didn't see me shake my head in answer to an assumption that Michael was listless.

"His appetite is off, is it not? He picks at his food?" More notations and still not glancing my direction. I pondered his ridiculous questions while trying to form an appropriate response—in case I ever had an opportunity to say something.

"He eats like a pig. Like always," I blurted out.

The doctors put their heads together.

"We concur. His spleen needs to be removed. The carbuncles? No doubt symptomatic," said the big cheese in charge.

"Symptomatic? Of what?" *Don't you dare tell me I don't keep him clean*!

"Can you bring your husband in with you? I need to speak with Sergeant Gill."

"No. Probably not. Why? Whatever it is, you can tell me."

That was not their anticipated response. They all stepped away from Michael and me and conversed for a few minutes. The colonel stepped back. I saw his eyes.

"We'll know more after his spleen is removed. Right now it looks like leukemia. Have you heard about leukemia? It's my duty to inform you we believe when it's caught this early it's treatable, but there's some urgency. Have your husband contact Colonel Hansen to give us his permission to operate. And don't you worry. We'll take good care of your little boy."

I anticipated a pat on my head, but it didn't come. But the doctor's condescending demeanor left me irate as he continued to talk down to me in front of his three mute underlings. My antennae stood at attention. In 1956 nearly everyone agreed that leukemia was untreatable and fatal. Now I knew why the doctors wanted me to agree to things that weren't true. Michael had to fit into a certain diagnosis and I didn't give the right answers so he ignored me.

I suspected the doctor wasn't above bullying me and I didn't trust him. As my mother used to say, 'my shackles were up.' My heart raced and I admit I was scared, and I thought: What if I'm wrong? What if Michael really does have leukemia? I heard Daddy's voice in my head. *When a salesman tries too hard to convince you that you can't live without it—whatever it is, step away, ask yourself why. If it's too good to be true, then it probably is.* I decided to step back.

No way was I going to allow this man with hard eyes to bamboozle me. I would let my intuition guide me. But for at least a half a minute I remained mute. Then I was a brazen Yankee woman who didn't know her place.

"You want to remove his spleen because he might have *blood cancer*? The sores on his scalp told you? The rest of the family has carbuncles. You don't suspect we all have leukemia, I mean blood cancer, do you?"

I knew he resented my impudence.

"That's right. Just the boy and it's rather serious. We'll do all we can to keep your son alive. You have your husband sign these papers tonight so we can set up the surgery as soon as possible. You should not delay it, trust me, time is of the essence."

All four men nodded. Realization hit me. *They need practice removing spleens. That's what this is about and why he tried to make me agree. Now I'm positive I can't trust these jokers.* I was young, female and small. They were twice my age, male and six feet tall, nearly a foot more than my five feet two inches.

Mother taught me that when men physically block my path I should simply outsmart them. I decided that applied to this situation and I smiled sweetly like the dummy they thought I was and accepted a card with the doctor's name, rank and telephone number on it. I promised to deliver the message to my husband and ask him to sign the necessary papers.

But my mind was made up. I wasn't bringing Michael back. If the carbuncles were to be cured, I'd do it. I'd rid us once and for all by boiling our linens or tossing them into the garbage and I'd liberally apply iodine and black Ichthyol ointment on everyone's sores. We could think about horrible diagnoses like leukemia later, if my burned-earth-take-no-prisoners effort failed and we were forced to.

Grandma Anderson had faith in a Seneca healer, my other grandmother saw the only doctor in town, Grandfather Fabian studied reports from the Government Printing Office and seldom sought additional medical advice, and both of my parents totally avoided hospitals and doctors, as I had until I met Bill. My birth family believed hospitals were where you went to die and that eighty percent of people who saw doctors really only needed somebody to listen to them.

Bill could continue to save the world, write duty rosters, assign latrine duties, and other important things like cheering hard for the Redskins and booing the Pirates. I tossed Colonel Hansen's message into the trash with contaminated bloody clothing.

Duty? I knew a thing or two about duty. I decided it was *my duty* to take care of the needs of this family to the point of daring to question a doctor's advice. And I did. My heart knew Michael didn't need his spleen removed, but convincing Bill wouldn't be easy. Going against the orders of WRAMC doctors would be difficult. I would be persuasive, but would he believe me? After serving dinner that night I told him what I wanted—no, needed to do.

"Before letting them operate on Michael let's go to Pennsylvania for a second opinion from my family doctor. He won't lie. I want to go to Erie. What do you say?"

"He's just a GP. He told you that before. He's not a specialist. Let's return to the docs at Walter Reed. They're experts. If taking out his spleen will save him from leukemia, we've got to do that. They said surgery. It's a waste of time to drive to Erie and it will cost a lot of money all for nothing."

"Maybe, but I don't believe Michael has leukemia. People die from that. He doesn't have the symptoms they want me to agree to. But if our family doctor concurs I'll agree to go back to WRAMC. I trust him. Please take me home. I'll ask Daddy for some gas money. Please? I don't consider it a waste of time. This is important to me."

"The docs at WRAMC are always right, Babe. But, okay. You win. We'll go."

It was an easier drive without a blizzard or a U-Haul-It trailer. The doctor saw us right away. Even if it didn't prove anything being there made me feel we had tried everything.

"We drove twelve hours to see you, doctor. I trust you more than the doctors at Walter Reed and I doubt their diagnosis. If you agree with them I'll quit stalling and agree to the surgery."

I explained the situation in more detail as he examined Michael. When he was finished, I quickly reiterated our willingness to do whatever he suggested.

"What do you think?"

"Well, I don't have fancy do-dads and equipment like they do at Walter Reed."

"But does he have symptoms of leukemia, blood cancer?"

"I don't see anything wrong with him except the sores, and you're doing the right thing about that. He perspires freely. That may encourage their growth and spread. Keep him as cool as you can, and keep him dry. I could be wrong, but I don't see *any* signs of leukemia. And I didn't feel an enlarged spleen. Unless it's an emergency I don't think removing the spleen of such a young child is even advisable."

On the way home I told Bill I wasn't giving my permission for a splenectomy and he should back me up. I knew he'd be reluctant to do that, but I had to ask.

"The Army doctors don't want to talk to me. You cancel our appointment. Colonel Hansen said he needed your consent, not mine... the chauvinist jerk."

"I can't argue about it. Doctor or not, he outranks me. It's my duty to obey officers."

"Nuts to that. Too much duty is bad for the soul!"

I didn't take Michael back to WRAMC, the carbuncle siege ended, and life settled into a comfortable routine. I visited back and forth with new friends, Marion and her daughter Peggy, six months younger than Mark, and six months older than Michael. They played together nearly every day while Peggy's mother and

I drank Pepsi from coffee cups so the children wouldn't know we were drinking taboo soft drinks. We shared our views on religion, child care, cooking, sewing, politics, and men. She and I were both from Pennsylvania, had married young and were happy stay-at-home moms. We talked, and laughed, and talked some more. Sometimes we gossiped about "Elvis the Pelvis." And I explained about carbuncles.

"They're not dangerous, unless you're diabetic, and they can be spread by runny noses or touching the sores. We treated them with soap and hot water. When a lot of them come at once it's called something else, but they're still ugly, pus filled carbuncles. I finally got rid of all of them and good riddance."

Two unrelated things happened after Valentine's Day. I realized I was pregnant again, and Bill announced he hated his job and had put in a 1049 transfer request listing San Antonio as number one on his dream sheet assuring me I'd love living in Texas.

"We'll visit Mexico. And The Alamo. Whatchasay, Babe? Great news, right?"

"Didn't you tell me you put in for a transfer to Fort Detrick, a few miles from here? Didn't we drive over there, and didn't you show me a cute little white cottage with a mossy green yard, and didn't you tell the kids we'd get a puppy? It'd be great for the boys. Now, you want to go to Texas? What happened to Fort Detrick and the puppy?"

Why does anyone want to move to Texas, when Fort Detrick is right here?

CHAPTER 17

Replacements

THE WORLD WAS moving forward and moving fast. To keep up with the times the Army made changes. By 1957 carrier pigeons had been eliminated in favor of more modern types of communication, the combat mule unit was replaced with helicopters allowing the first helicopter unit to be activated at Fort Bragg, North Carolina, and at Redstone Arsenal, Alabama the first Ballistic Missile Agency was established. It was rumored the M-14 would replace the M-1 rifle, BAR and M-1 carbine. When the new green uniform was introduced "the old brown shoes Army" went out, and "the new black shoes Army" came in. Changes in the Regular Army occurred faster than most could keep up, and if I recall correctly the Veterinary Service, still active in medical battalions, was on the way out. Reservists who had been called up to fight in Korea were being returned to civilian life—often unwillingly. The Army was modernizing.

Upgraded MOS (job description) skills and cross training became important to soldiers who wanted to stay in the Army. As a medic trained at Brooke, in San Antonio, Bill's assignments were limited by his MOS. He decided to get promoted he would have to attend advanced dental technician's school making him not only a trained medic but also a dental lab technician (dental hygienist) thereby doubling his opportunity for assignments and promotions and assuring him that he was safe from riffing.

Bill said he'd seen the writing on the wall and if he wanted good assignments he needed to acquire more training. He spent weeks trying to convince me to move to Texas. He planned to keep enlisting every six years until he had served twenty or thirty years and could retire. He needed more training.

It was true that Army life and the world around us had changed since the end of World War and The Conflict in Korea. The first nuclear power reactor was dedicated at Fort Belvoir in April and a few months later President Eisenhower sent the 101st Airborne Division and Arkansas National Guard to Little Rock to enforce school integration. On any given day military families lived twenty years ahead of the civilian population; we didn't realize that until much later, but we all tried to keep abreast of the news.

Bill aspired to being a "lifer" and was ready to work hard and sacrifice to obtain that goal. Going to Texas for additional training was part of a long range plan. He was quite undiplomatic in explaining those plans to me.

"It's a done deal, Babe. Gotta keep on my toes. I've already received orders. I'm going. So are you. You can live off post while I go to school and afterward I request duty there, we get government quarters, and we stay! Babe, I can hardly wait. You're going to love Texas."

Remember that I like to plan in advance, but Bill was a spur of the moment guy. Sometimes we clashed. This would be one of those times. This would require careful balancing. This time it wouldn't be the Carolina Shuffle, it would be an adagio dance.

A strong man needs a strong woman. I didn't look strong, but when Richard died I discovered how resilient I was and that I was made of sterner stuff perhaps stainless steel where it counts on the inside. In other words, I have a strong personality and character to the core. Bill has, too. He was a popular, fierce leader and other strong men were willing to follow him on the football

102

field or the battlefield and he was the type everyone respected and obeyed. He was unaccustomed to anyone questioning his leadership, his desires or challenging his goals. But I was a gutsy girl and I wouldn't be pushed around. I refused to move to Texas.

The ball was in Bill's court. What would he do?

CHAPTER 18

—— ⚘ ——

Baby Talk

"COME ON, HONEY. Texas is wonderful. The kids can get a horse or a pony instead of a puppy."

"I don't get it. We've only lived here since July. That's less than a year!"

"Yeah, Babe. I know. But we're moving to Texas. He-haw, San An-tone! I need to take an advanced course at Brooke. I'm doing it for you, Babe. Trust me."

"Ha! You said you wanted to be assigned to *this* area and were happy to be here. We've only lived here a few months. What happened?"

"I'm mal assigned. I need to move out, get away from WRAMC, pdq. Before I go nuts. Being in D.C. again is great, but my job here is way out of my MOS (job description). I guess I need more training to get a shot at a better assignment."

"What about the kids? And don't claim you're doing it for me! What about me?"

"What about you? This doesn't concern you, Babe."

Oh, really? It doesn't concern me?

"How about that place near here? What happened with that? I liked the looks of those little white bungalows and the lawns are so pretty, like a golf course."

"I found out something. They do a lot of secret experimental things there. I don't think I want to be part of all that cloak and dagger stuff. Fact is, I don't. I told them thanks, but no thanks. I turned down the Detrick transfer. I'm not interested in working with....whatever it is they do. We're going to go to Texas, maybe buy a house, settle down and retire there. It's not up for debate."

In my mind's eye I wore black tights, shirt, black spike three inch heels and a beret. I carried a long stem red rose between my front teeth. Let the slow music start. Let the dance begin.

"Well, I'm not excited about moving already. And my doctor will discourage it."

"Ah, Babe. You look great. The doc will say it's fine. Anyway, we're moving to Texas."

"I don't want to."

The next day I made another appointment at the OB/GYN Clinic at WRAMC. Based on my medical history and my current physical problem, delivering a healthy baby seemed unlikely. The doctor warned me I'd probably miscarry if I wasn't willing to stay in bed for the first trimester.

Bill refused to discuss my medical condition or accept it as a reason to remain at WRAMC, but he said he was willing to help with the house work and would do all the packing. And he was still insisting we were moving to Texas.

Bill was at work before the boys got up and didn't return until two hours before their bedtime. I knew I could lie on the sofa and keep an eye on them while we all watched Captain Kangaroo, but I began to depend of Marion's daily visit and help in the afternoon because Bill wasn't really available.

I hated being a twenty-three year old invalid. I phoned WRAMC and asked the doctor if I *really had to stay in bed*. Maybe he'd change his prognosis.

"It's been a week. I feel okay."

"Okay. Get up, don't have a baby. Or, stay on your back like I said. It's your choice."

Bill came home early wearing a big smile which I ignored. How dare he be happy when the doctor had just squashed my dreams? I pictured myself in my black outfit still adagio dancing and ready for a fight to the finish.

I said, "I'm hungry. What's for supper? That's why you're home early, isn't it? What's so funny? Why are you laughing? The kitchen's there—that way!"

"Yeah. Ha! Ha! You're a riot, Babe. But get this. It's all set."

I suspected what was coming next and flexed my toes inside my dancing shoes fairly certain the tempo was about to increase from lento. The fight was on. En garde!

"What's set? You're going… somewhere? Where...are you going?"

"No. We are. To San An-tone. Hee-haw! I can't wait. We'll leave soon as you pack."

"Impossible. I can't pack or go that far. Not during the first trimester!"

"Orders are orders, Babe. We'll take it slow. I don't report for three weeks. You'll be fine. Call the doc in the morning. Ask him. He's Regular Army. He'll understand."

I repeated the doctor's warning about losing the baby. I again said no to Texas.

"Oh, he said all that? I didn't know it was serious. I just thought…"

"Yeah? What did you think? You thought I wanted attention? I was faking?"

"Something like that. I've known women who acted like that. And you look okay."

"Sure you know women who fake it. Like your own mother, maybe? You think I'm just like your mother? Faking it? This is life and death, Will-i-am! Don't you get it? I *can't* get up and do things. If I do, this baby will become a miscarriage!"

"Yeah, well sometimes Mom fakes it, but she's always been kindly sickly, according to her brother, Abraham. Aw, Babe. Let's not fight. You're not a bit like her. Come here, I've got something for you."

I felt his arms around me and we swayed back and forth. Gone were the fighting adagio dancers. It was the Carolina Shuffle. In a moment I said I had to lie down.

About the same time we heard the familiar ding-a-ling-ling of the Good Humor ice cream truck. You could say we were saved by the bell.

"Will you go out and get us some ice cream?"

"Sure Babe. What do you and the boys want?"

"I don't care."

"You gotta say something. If I go out there with a stupid I don't care attitude, that guy won't give me nothing! What do you want?"

"Banana splits. We want to share two banana splits."

While we enjoyed eating ice cream I brought up the topic of ranks and promotions. How was I to know it would cause Bill to get upset and yell at me? I only asked when he might get promoted.

"I met a lady at the OB/GYN Clinic. She was waiting to see a doctor, too and we got to talking. Her husband was just promoted to sergeant first class. When will you get promoted to sergeant first class?"

I licked my sticky fingers and put my ice cream dish on the end table beside the sofa.

Through tightly clenched teeth Bill informed me he was already a master sergeant.

"Master sergeant is as high as it goes! I'm already higher than a sergeant first class."

"Oh. Well, okay. No need to yell. It seemed to me that sergeant first class should be higher, but if you say so....I guess you should know."

The next day he phoned to ask if I could ride as far as Fort Jackson, South Carolina. *Wow! That was* a *fast change.* The adagio music in my head stopped.

"I don't know, I'll ask the doctor. Why?"

When Marion came to help watch the boys I told her we'd be moving soon to Fort Jackson, South Carolina near Columbia. We promised each other we'd stay in touch. She said they'd visit us on summer vacation.

Bill handled the details for shipping our household goods and packing the car. He promised we would stop to rest along the way, but we didn't stop until Statesville, three hours north of Fort Jackson. I felt physically fine, but not emotionally. I was very worried about losing our baby. I'd had to put my life and the life of my unborn in jeopardy for something I thought was an avoidable peril. I also resented having to visit his relatives in the middle of our move.

As it turned out, and much to Bill's surprise and mine, his father took pity on me and scolded Bill. We were in the backyard and I was chatting with Mister Gill. Bill sneaked up behind me and dropped an ice-cube down the back of my maternity smock causing me to shriek in surprise and jump from my Adirondack chair. His father yelled at Bill in tones and words I never dreamed he would use on his only son, the person he doted on.

"Son! Don't you *ever* do such a thing like that again!"

He said that with the voice of authority giving me the idea his time in The Philippines during World War II had taught him a few things. Now he was my hero!

By the end of March I knew the danger had passed and the baby was safe. We moved into a cute little brick duplex off post near the Main Gate. I felt well, but not strong. Definitely not strong enough to fend off an army of huge roaches that were trying to take over our house.

I believed clean people didn't have cockroaches. Not where I was reared. I believed they were only found among the poorest, uneducated, dirtiest people and I wasn't lowering my standards to fit into that category. Not ever. The house was fine, but I didn't plan to live in it.

"I refuse to live like this, Will-i-am. I won't, I won't, I won't. Do something, Sergeant Gill! The bugs are trying to take over and I can't stand it!"

Bill brought home a white powder Post Engineers cautioned would kill the kids if they ate it. I sprinkled it behind the piano and other places kids couldn't reach and watched as those despicable roaches paraded across the green living room carpet displaying white powder all over their backs. I swear they gave me the rasp-berry—a Bronx cheer--as they passed in review. Bill wasn't nearly as concerned about the roaches as I was. It was going to be up to me to get rid of them.

I read all I could find about roaches and learned scientists ex-pect them to outlive everything else on earth. *Well, good for them, but not in my house!* The fight was on. It was them or me. While implementing an extermination plan I intended to be merciless. If I opened a drawer and one jumped out it died a loud crunchy death beneath my shoe. I searched out roaches in every nook or cranny and attacked them with a generous spray from a can of poison. Oh, I was ruthless, but they were brazen beyond my wildest imagination. In bed I clutched a large flashlight all night hoping to head off adven-turous night crawling roaches. I killed dozens of invaders, but when reinforcements arrived I threw up my hands in defeat. I didn't want to fight any longer. I was outnumbered. They won. I surrendered.

"You can have the house," I shouted at the walls where they nested. "You win!" I opened the phone book to the Yellow pages and ran my finger down the list of realtors.

That night as soon as Bill came in the door I said, "We need to move. Immediately."

"We just moved in here. I've got a little money. Call Otto the Orkin Man again."

"No. His extermination stuff didn't work. I will not live in this roach palace!"

"Where do you want to live, Babe? In South Carolina big roaches live in the grass right outside the door. They waltz back in as soon as Otto leaves. He even told you that. Get used to it. You can't get rid of them."

"I can! And I have to. My parents are on the way to visit us!"

"So?"

"So? That's what you say? So? I'm going out. I'll find a realtor with a house to rent. You stay home and babysit the roaches." I picked up my purse and his car keys.

"Wait, Babe. I promise. Tomorrow we'll find a different place to live."

Tomorrow got postponed for some reason and it was two weeks before we found a new house. In the meantime my mother and father had a vacation they never forgot. I wasn't surprised when Daddy announced they'd be going home early. Mother and Daddy had sat up all night with the lights on. I explained about Otto, and the white powdery poison from the Army Engineers, and the bugs living outside the door, but I was wasting my breath, and I knew it.

Mother said, "Interesting." I can't repeat what Daddy had to say about the entire situation.

The evening after my parents left I laid down an ultimatum. "Move us, or else!"

"We'll discuss it tomorrow. I've got the duty tonight at the dental clinic."

I was fuming mad and didn't really believe his excuse, but didn't care. I used the time to pack our things. One way or another, the kids and I would no longer reside in cockroach paradise. If Bill didn't come with us, so be it. We'd go alone.

The next day we both met with a realtor who apparently didn't like Yankees, or maybe only uppity Yankee women, like me. When riled I'm a force to fear, a mama bear with Swedish Viking blood on the verge of berserking. I *appear to be* brave. I'm really scared silly and shaking internally, but formidable and determined. Determined women are dangerous. That's how I felt when we met the realtor. Dangerous.

"You best be gittin' used ta dem, you live in da south, Mizzrus. Everbody gots 'em."

"Not me," I said as decisively as a Joe Louis haymaker. "If you'll fumigate the house today we'll take it!"

"Drives a hard bargain don' she? Sergeant, y'all shu 'bout dis?"

Daddy taught me to never be a door mat for anybody, not ever. I guess he'd be proud the way I put my foot down that day. I know I was. I waited to see what Bill would do.

"Well? Will-i-am? Tell him," I said dripping sarcasm. "Are you?" *He better say yes.*

"Yeah. Do as the little lady says. We'll take it. I'm sure as a heart attack. Gimme a pen and show me where to sign."

Bill said he loved me from the first moment because I had a mind of my own and wasn't a shy shrinking violet like other girls he knew. I hoped after today that he'd still feel the same.

"It's my duty tell y'all, lease's only good 'til he comes back from overseas."

While Bill signed I turned on my heel and stomped to the car.

The three bedroom white frame house stood on a sandy hill in a thickly wooded area near Fort Jackson's Gate Three. Nobody mentioned snakes to me, and I didn't think about them. All I cared about at the time was roaches. I slammed the car door for emphasis.

CHAPTER 19

❦

Homesteaders

About three o'clock the morning of October second the following year our only daughter, Linda Sue, was born in a frame structure —one passing as the Army hospital at Fort Jackson, South Carolina—a building that might have been a barracks during "the war," meaning World War II. True to traditional military medical care the doctor on call was one I hadn't met and after he ordered a saddle block anesthesia, never saw again. Rows of single beds in the make-shift, crowded facility lined the walls in close proximity to each other and provided negligible privacy. Was it really a World War II Quonset hut? Did I dream it? After the delivery I wasn't sure,couldn't remember. I did remember that I didn't ever want another saddle block anesthesia.

When he came to visit Bill cupped his hand around his mouth and whispered, "You get the name of the woman in the next bed?"

I was curious, but still groggy. I slurred my words. "In the next bed? Yeah. I think it's something Italian. Maybe Pellegrino. Why?" My eyes were too heavy to hold open.

"Never mind. Our baby looks great. I'll be back after I call every-one. Give me a kiss."

I think I kissed him, but like I said, it was an ethereal experience.

The next few weeks were reasonably normal, if that can ever be said of an Army family. My parents and Aunt Elda came to visit. And because of hard feelings after their divorce Bill's parents refused to come together and took turns visiting.

The third week in November we drove to Erie to show off our daughter, for Turkey Day, and to celebrate Daddy's fifty-seventh birthday. The night we arrived there wasn't a snowflake in sight but during the night that changed. In the morning I couldn't identify which hump of the white stuff in front of the house hid our car. Roads were impassable and closed by executive order forcing Bill to request an emergency extension to his leave. After a bright sun caused crusted snow to sparkle like diamonds, snow kept falling and Mark and Mike played in drifts deeper than they were tall.

Plows finally arrived and cleared the roads enough for the governor to allow traffic to flow again and we headed south on slippery two-lane highways. When the car heater failed causing the formula in Linda's baby bottles to freeze solid we were forced to detour, stop, and lay-over at Molly's Bed and Breakfast near Berkley Springs in the hills of West Virginia.

A few months later we planted a garden, put up a small picket fence, got a cocker spaniel and named him Patrick. Bill successfully underwent knee surgery to repair torn cartilage. I had begun to think of us as homesteaders until one day during Lent Bill announced he had put in a 1049 transfer request listing Alaska number one on his dream sheet. Shocked, I asked why. I thought he was happy at Jackson.

"Been here over two years, Babe. Too long. Time to boogie on down the road."

"We're all settled. We've got friends here. I don't get it."

"Yeah, we're real homesteaders. I'm not cut out for homesteading."

"Linda is eighteen months old, the boys are nearly pre-school. What about them?"

"We can drive cross country. Do a ton of sightseeing. Maybe I can do a little bear hunting, see Kodiak? It's a chance to see the last frontier before it's gone. It'll be a great experience for the kids, one they won't forget. You said you wanted to see Alaska."

"Yeah, sure. I wanted to move to Australia, but you didn't do anything about that!"

He unlaced his steel toed boots and kicked them off as the boys scrambled to see who would be first to rub his feet and earn a nickel.

"Well, I sent off the request. I guess now we just wait for orders."

"What about the kids and me? Where do we go?"

"I asked for accompanied, so it will be a three year tour. Y'all are coming with me. Read up on polar bears and Eskimos."

"And you can read up on how to be a father to four kids. I'm expecting again. I had a baby in an old hotel in Stuttgart, and one in a Quonset hut, but I'm not going to have a baby in an igloo! I won't change my mind, Will-i-am! Are you paying attention? Do you hear me? No babies in igloos!"

That summer of 1959 Bill's relatives gave us bushels of tomatoes and peaches. July was a scorcher and I was in advanced pregnancy unhappily sweating over a canner in our oppressively hot kitchen. I grew sick of looking at peaches and moved to the living room to sit with my swollen feet submerged in a galvanized bucket of cold water and a borrowed fan blowing hot air on me. I felt fat, like I was burning up, and miserable. After two days of 103 degrees, *in the shade* according to our outdoor thermometer, Alaska was looking better and better.

It had become nearly impossible to see over my extended belly. Maybe the doctor and I miscalculated. Was this baby due in

August? There was about as much chance of that as getting ice tea in Hades. I was sure the September payday was the due date.

I couldn't bend over to pack anything, but I did mentally start sorting what to take on the inevitable move from one extreme climate to the opposite. Sandals and sunsuits would go into a carton to give away.

When orders finally arrived they weren't for Alaska but for a place not even listed on the dream sheet. And the orders were for an *unaccompanied* one year tour not a three year accompanied like Bill expected. He was going to the demilitarized zone (DMZ), 38th parallel, South Korea!

After talking myself into going with him into the wilds of Alaska he wasn't going.

"I'm as shocked as you, Babe. But at least it's a good assignment."

"But, southeast Asia? Again?"

If I'd known he was a future sergeant major striving to get ahead I might have felt differently. But try, as I did, I couldn't share his enthusiasm.

"For a whole year? By yourself? What about us?"

During the 1951 fighting in Korea Bill was offered a battlefield commission but declined. He told me he'd said, 'Thank you sir, but no sir. I'll just rotate in a couple months with both arms and legs and wearing three up and three down. I'll be going home and I don't expect ever to see this hell-hole again.' Now, seven years later, he was willingly returning to Korea because he put in a volunteer request to go to Alaska. Go figure! Bill's dream sheet had just become my nightmare sheet.

"What happens to us while you're gone? We have to live somewhere!"

I knew the owner of our house was coming home soon. Where would we live while Bill was overseas? I knew he expected me to say

I'd go live with my parents again, but that wasn't going to happen. I'd have to rent a house in Erie if I wanted to live near my family and I really didn't want to go back north. My friends were here now, not even my childhood best friend would be in Erie. Her husband had been transferred to Livermore, California.

Bill's totally unexpected response floored me and left me temporarily speechless.

"You can join me there, but then I have to stay three years. We could live in quarters in Seoul. Or, I can go by myself and come back in one year. Your choice, Babe."

My choice? Oh, yeah. Sure it is. That would be a change. Ha! Ha!

"Well, since you're leaving I need to ask a doctor at Jackson to check the due date. My legs and arms are skinny, but look at my belly! When I tried to drive I couldn't fit behind the wheel. I'm huge! Don't I look ready to pop right now? Don't answer that!"

"I ship out fifteen October, Babe. I hear it's nice for families in Seoul."

"I hear it's close to North Koreans. Call somebody and get your orders changed."

"Hell, no," he said ending the conversation. He was *anxious* to go to Korea!

Army wives have long suspected soldier husbands of having a secret pact with the Pentagon allowing husbands to ship out at opportune times—like when a baby is due. Bill's sudden change of orders enforced that conspiracy theory but didn't explain why he was happy about it. What did Korea have that Alaska lacked? What did he know about it that he wasn't telling me?

In a few days I went to the OB/GYN clinic. The doctor I saw that time suggested taking my picture. He meant an X-Ray. It revealed two babies. We were having identical twin sons! When asked if twins ran in our families I admitted I didn't know but thought Grandfather Anderson did have twin brothers, but I'd ever seen them.

"Twins often happen in families with no history of multiples. Nothing to fret about."

"My husband's on overseas orders. I'm going to Pennsylvania to live near my family. Should I plan to fly?"

"Absolutely not! If you go into labor in the air the pilot won't land the plane for you. You go by car and make a note of the name of each town you pass in case you need a hospital. Leave as soon as possible. Twins usually arrive at least two weeks early."

This new information changed our plans. Bill was excited and solicitous of my health. This wasn't an ordinary situation. He notified everyone he could think of that we expected twin boys dramatically elevating his status among some of his colleagues.

We left Jackson September fifteenth, 1959, on the exact date the doctor said the twins might arrive. The sun rose as we crossed into Virginia and I prayed we'd arrive in Erie without car trouble or labor pains and very thankful for the cooler temperature as we drove north.

I felt as comfortable as I could be considering my condition because Bill was driving the two-year old green and white station wagon we recently bought in Columbia, South Carolina instead of our unreliable old '49 Chevy coupe.

One day on our way to Sears the Chevy had chugged, coughed, and stopped. When it refused to start up after coughing to a halt we knew it had given up the ghost; it was dead. Bill shoved it out of gear and into neutral and we coasted into the first dealership's lot that we saw.

Daddy would have repaired it with chewing gum, string and imagination but car repair was not one of Bill's skills and

Daddy was in Pennsylvania. Making it worse, the horn began be-e-e-ping without stopping and a seedy looking guy with greasy hair and wearing a blue and white suit saw us and headed our way.

"Get your Yankee horse trading skills out, Babe. Now! We're trading cars."

I felt out of place in a blue dotted swiss church dress, white pumps, and white lace mitts that I wore because we had intended to shop and eat dinner in Columbia. Buying a car had not been on my shopping list, and I didn't feel like haggling.

Bill jumped out leaving me to follow as he sauntered over to shake hands with the sleazy guy in the seersucker suit. I guess I had horse trading skills, but Bill had the palaver of a born politician and in a few minutes the two men acted like they were old buddies. After I joined them we talked an hour before the man irked me.

"Don't worry about having your name on the title, little lady. South Carolina has the dowry law, Sugah. That means if he dies, God forbid, you automatically get a third of everything."

"Sorry, Harry. If my husband dies I intend to inherit *everything*. I want my name on the title or it's no sale." Bill agreed. That settled we signed papers and drove away in our new car.

It was a strange way to buy a car but fortunate for us that the Chevy died there instead of on the way to Erie. The station wagon gave ample room for everyone including our dog, Patrick, who liked to ride in the tailgate area and bark at cars behind us. It was more comfortable than the Chevy but the drive from South Carolina to Pennsylvania would have been miserable in any car packed to capacity with clothes, toys, three small children, a barking dog, and a miserable overdue pregnant woman.

We watched for hospital signs and noted the distance to the nearest one—just in case. I didn't go into labor until two weeks later at St. Vincent's Hospital in Erie where a kind nun made the mistake of admitting Bill to the labor room. I was surprised to see him there because he believed, like many men, that birthing was for women and fathers were only expected to nervously pace the halls, buy flowers, and give out cigars.

Bill wanted to help me but had no idea what to do. He began telling stupid jokes.

"Not funny, Will-i-am!" He made a sad face and began again. "This is no joke!"

I couldn't stand it, or him. I yelled for the nurse. "G-g-g-et him out of h-h-h-ere!" It was the first time I had ever stuttered. Bill was happy to go and I was relieved that he was gone.

Much, much later I understood that Bill joked in order to hide his feeling of helplessness. As the Pennsylvania Dutch say: Vee git too soon aldt, und too late schmart.

A nurse reminded me to pant like a dog to help hurry it along and between contractions I reminisced. That's why I remembered my broken toe. That had hurt, too.

༄

The day of the toe brouhaha Bill had come home in his usual fatigues and heavy black combat boots. He roughhoused with the boys a while then grabbed the newspaper to read, but they wanted to continue playing. Mark ran toward him to be caught and held high in the air to simulate flying. Mike followed suit and each did it several times. From where I stood in the kitchen doorway it looked like fun. I decided to try it.

I ran toward Bill hollering for him to catch me and was airborne when I heard him say, "No, Babe. Watch out! Don't. Not yet!" His warning came too late and I crashed smacking my bare foot full force into the steel toe of Bill's boot. I collapsed on the carpet, rolled into the fetal position, and howled bloody blue murder.

"Ow, ow, ow! Help, help, help! Oh, oh, oh. My toe, my toe, my toe! I've killed it!"

"Quit kidding around, honey. I wasn't ready for you. Want to try it again?"

Alan Alda's television program M.A.S.H. was set in a surgical field hospital in Korea where doctors, corpsmen, nurses—every-body-- played pranks and laughed as a defense mechanism. Bill grew that kind of rhinoceros hide to protect his emotions after witnessing buddies die in combat, their bodies blown to bits. He wasn't unkind to me, but he was immune to anything he deemed not life threatening. The day I broke my toe he thought I was put-ting on a show, kidding around. I had to make him realize that I was genuinely injured. And it really, truly hurt.

"No joke. Look! I killed my toe. Take me to the hospital." I sobbed big, fat tears.

"Come on, Hot Lips." Bill carried me into the bathroom, sat me on the edge of the tub, and turned on the faucet. He lifted my foot and held it under the cold water.

"All better?"

"No-o-o-o-o-. Can't you see? It's turned around going the wrong direction!"

"You're right, Babe. That's one crazy looking toe! I'll fix that in a jiffy."

My toe was repositioned with a quick jerk. My sudden deluge of tears surprised him.

"See? It isn't going the wrong way now. Uh, don't move. I'll be right back, Babe."

He returned holding a frozen orange popsicle and stuck half in his mouth and ordered me to eat the other half. I didn't want it, but I obeyed. He took the stick, licked it clean, broke it in half, applied both pieces to my toe creating a splint, and wrapped it with white gauze.

"Good as new," he said.

Bill was wrong about that. I limped like a little old lady for the next dozen weeks. But I didn't know for sure it had been broken until a doctor asked during a routine exam to explain how I broke it. Trying to think up an answer that didn't make me sound flaky, I omitted the part about flying and hitting a combat boot. I told him I tripped and stubbed my toe. But now it was time to concentrate on having twins and forget about broken toes.

There are two types of people. One, like my husband, is the type I want with me in event of a crisis like an enemy attack. The other is slow moving, thoughtful and steady. I hoped my new doctor was type two, not the type to suture me with whatever was handy, like Bill would.

When I arrivedin Lawrence Park nine months pregnant and without a doctor my childhood best friend, Pati, had recommended Dr. Peterson. As a favor to her he had accepted me as his patient. He said Baby A (Robert) and Baby B (Thomas) had a combined birth weight of eleven pounds and eleven ounces and both were healthy.

Bill gave out cigars and went shopping at The Boston Store for a second layette. Fortunately, he couldn't exactly duplicate A's outfits from the PX at Jackson, and the boys began life as individuals— a good thing—as soon as they were born.

Two weeks passed. Bill left us in a rented house a block from my parents' and shipped out to the DMZ for a year. This time neighbors expected him to return. I wasn't so sure. A parent might *want* to escape. I couldn't. Somebody had to stay home and take care of five pre-school-age children and everything else. That's what Army wives do. So that's what I did while Bill was gone.

Look on a map or check with Google. You'll see that Bill fled 6,673 miles to the other side of the world to escape from us. I'm kidding about that, he really didn't run away from us, but it was hectic living in snow country with infant twins, a toddler, and two small children the winter of 1959-60 and I wouldn't have blamed him if he had.

A letter arrived one chaotic afternoon. I read: *Babe, I can get us a house in the capital city complete with servants. And didn't you say you wanted to go to China after you read Pearl Buck's book, The Good Earth? Maybe we could. Please come here. I'm being bored to death staring at North Koreans staring back at me!*

He was right about Pearl Buck's story about old China. It did inspire me to visit China, but it was too late. The China she described was gone, replaced with communism. I wrote back using a roll of toilet tissue for stationery and gave a scathing description of a day in the life of five babies and their mother explaining why I wasn't traveling to Korea. Not ever. Neither would I ever visit China or see the Pacific Ocean. Was he insane to think it was even possible?

I wrote: *I've lost weight while gobbling chocolates between meals; none of my clothes fit. Just getting through mealtime is an endeavor weaker people shouldn't try. Nobody can cut up their own food, nobody can use a fork. Everybody spills milk at least once a day,.etc. And laundry? Let's not talk about how many Birdseye cotton diapers I change, tubs of them I wash and hang outdoors where they freeze into solid white squares. Those diapers will make good dust rags in the future. This year? I don't have time to dust. I saw a rat on the back porch and our supposed watch dog refused to go outside. I phoned the State Police to ask for help, but was told*

"There are no rats in this township!" *I have my hands full. PS Have you gone mad? Or drunk on Saki? Asking me to travel thousands of miles alone with five little kids? I think you must be* nuts. (signed) *your loving wife,* followed by a row of Xs and Os.

The station wagon remained snowed in in the garage until mid-April. Lacking a car but not stamina I mushed to the grocery store dragging the twins and Linda on an old toboggan while Mark and Mike in red rubber boots and snowsuits ran circles around us and threw snowballs at each other.

I hoped to carve tranquility from chaos, stability from disorder, steadfastness from continual change, but we, like Lake Erie, were never still. Staying on course during squalls kept our deceptively perfect family from being sucked under by dangerous undertows in the shoals and with the help of prayer we avoided SNAFU experiences, but I couldn't avoid change. Change followed us around like a new puppy.

CHAPTER 20

— ❧ —

To Move or Not To Move

ONE AUGUST MORNING I answered the stylish green wall phone Uncle Gurth had given us, but I didn't recognize the professional voice of the male caller or his name when he gave it. Had change found me?

"This is Doctor John Harvey Nicholson. The Red Cross is bringing Bill home," he said.

"Why? Is he sick? Wounded? He's dead? What happened to him?"

"No. Nothing like that. It's because I'm his father's doctor and his father had another massive heart attack. I need permission to give him an experimental drug. Bill's his only child and next of kin, but unavailable until it may be too late. Will you give it?"

"Me? You want *me* to give permission? What if I don't?"

"Bill's father dies."

I'm a realist. It took seconds to assess the situation and make a decision.

"Give him the drug and tell him the kids and I will arrive in Statesville tomorrow."

Patricia, a longtime friend, happened to drop by as I was packing to leave. "You can't do this by yourself," she said.

Patricia insisted on going with us to help drive to North Carolina. We were ready to leave by noon but I was worried about Thomas who was wrapped in a wool crib blanket over his clothes because he had been sick—probably because of hay fever allergies—but

I was concerned enough to check with his doctor before leaving Pennsylvania.

"Thomas can be sick in the car, or North Carolina as well as here. Go," he said.

The weather stayed bright and sunny but it was a long trip that seemed longer in spite of Patricia's help because going from Erie to Statesville with five little kids in the car is, well, difficult. We arrived at Eva's apartment on Kelly Street about the same time Bill arrived from Korea.

While getting ready to go to the hospital to visit Mr. Gill I asked Bill if he had to return to Korea. When he said no I hoped we'd move to D.C. near Marion again.

"I've been assigned to Fort Lee, Virginia south of Richmond. I think it's an E-8 slot."

"Oh. Is Fort Lee near Washington?"

"No. Not really. But an E-8 slot means a promotion, Babe. And a pay raise."

"Oh," I slid behind the steering wheel to drive us to Iredell Memorial Hospital.

"Move over, honey. It's too much for you. I'm home now. I'll do the driving."

How come I'm capable of doing everything all year, but not now? I moved over.

The experimental medicine let Mr. Gill rally making me glad I had said to give it to him. I wondered why his wife, Grace, wasn't the one asked, but I never knew. We remained several days after Patricia returned to Erie by air and Bill helped his beloved father recuperate. Soon it was time to go north and tell my folks about our pending move to Fort Lee.

This move would be hard on the older kids. They felt at home near Erie in bucolic little Lawrence Park Township and had begun putting down roots. They saw people like their grandparents and classmates didn't live like gypsies, like we did.

Our kids, devoted little Army brats, seemed to thrive on our nomadic lifestyle. I tried to convince myself that what they learned from moving about the world would prove invaluable in their futures. They would meet and know Michiko, a beautiful model from Kyoto, and a white Russian who escaped the Revolution and later married an American soldier. They would play with Japanese and British children and understand international politics better than their peers. Our neighbors might be from Cleveland, Seoul, Reno, Detroit, London, Beirut, or Tokyo and our kids would learn geography, discover other cultures, and learn languages from native speakers. They would experience the School of Hard Knocks and also public/private schools. At home I would continue to provide an introduction to the arts, including music, needlecrafts, drawing, debate, manners, and language skills. By the time they were ready for college, would any American college be ready for them? What an education they'd have!

Indeed, the Army lifestyle sometimes feels like a hard row to hoe, but the benefits are huge. Because of the Army we had food, clothing, shelter and boundless opportunities. Was that enough or was it time for *me* to change? I knew sergeants had a high rate of divorce and for some reason they also had more kids than any rank. I wondered how those kids fared and whether or not I should drag ours from pillar to post until Bill retired. Was it time to refuse to move? Had change found us again?

Finally, after prayer, debate, and with trepidation, I agreed to move to Fort Lee, near Hopewell, Virginia and the James River. It was a sad day when I told my parents we'd be leaving and I saw they were not very happy about it and were aging, but at least this time Daddy believed he'd see us again. He was his old smiling self, standing on the porch and waving but I knew he felt miserable because saying good-bye to someone you love is always hard.

Daddy promised the first time they came to visit he'd bring cuttings of his rose bushes. "And I'll plant them for you," he said. He also gave Thomas a cutting to take in the car to our new home making it possible to keep a little bit of Lawrence Park with us.

Fifteen hours later when we reached Fort Lee I was tired. But not too tired to admire the new townhouse assigned to us on Cherbourg Lane at the end of a row, in a quiet, clean area boasting clipped green lawns. Once inside, I was thrilled to find a modern kitchen with all new appliances, a powder room downstairs, and a full bath upstairs. We moved in quickly—as we always did, and adjusted to the rhythm of our new community.

It was the end of August and time for Mark and Michael to be in school. But when we tried to take the boys there--elated to hear there was an elementary school on post--my happiness was short-lived. The Fort Lee Elementary School had been closed with no plans to ever open and many public schools across Virginia also remained closed because of race riots and racial tension.

I suggested taking our kids back to Pennsylvania, but Bill asked somebody where other military children were enrolled and learned they went to a parochial school in Hopewell, Virginia, a small town near The James River. He arranged—how remains mysterious—to get our boys admitted there. The second piece of good news was an Army shuttle bus stopped across the street from our quarters and would take them to and from school each day.

That settled, I waved a magic wand and began to transfer "home" from Pennsylvania to Fort Lee by relocating a small table and little chairs to the kitchen where I created what I dubbed "Kitchengarten" as a replacement for unavailable public kindergarten. Next, and with help from the entire family, I supervised the transformation of every inch of our new home to make it look and feel familiar and provide some stability. Everyone helped as I strategically arranged furniture and accessories we dragged from station to station. Why? I hoped this effort would psychologically provide a modicum of continuity and maintaining semblance of a stable home whether in a foreign country, a tent, or government quarters at Fort Lee, is important and because that's what Army wives do.

CHAPTER 21

Teaching and Learning

As St. James' school in Hopewell tried to accommodate desperate parents by admitting sixty children to classrooms designed for only thirty, teaching Sisters and laity were short of supplies and overworked. Race riots forced additional school closings in Virginia and Mark and Michael entered first and second grades.

In high school I had had two hours of art instruction with Miss Sack every day. I wasn't a budding Van Gogh, but I did have enough basic skills to teach drawing and coloring in grades one through six. Only one nun raised a negative voice and complained that art was a waste of time.

"It makes us look like a public school," she said frowning.

During Lent I helped students draw a rabbit and asked them to color it. I walked up and down the aisles stopping often to admire their work. A disturbance in the back of the room attracted my attention. Sister B. was scolding someone. I hurried to her side in time to hear the nun roundly berate a boy because he had colored his rabbit bright red. Oh, oh! Did I want to side with him and cross Sister B., a self-declared former Army brat? It was, after all, a creative writing class and he had nicely colored within the lines.

Procrastinating, or simply hoping for divine intervention, I decided to ask a question.

"Is that a real bunny?"

Keeping his eyes downcast he said, "No, ma'am. It's my toy bun-ny rabbit."

Without a word the nun folded her hands inside her black habit, about-faced so perfectly she would have been envied by the cadre, and ramrod straight she clomped down the aisle.

"Red's a wonderful color for a toy rabbit," I said when she was out of range.

The fourth grade teacher fell ill and there was no replacement available until Bill volunteered. He took a thirty day leave and substi-tuted until the teacher returned. Bill loved every minute of his ten-ure as a teacher and initiated the Army's Physical Training Program (Pre-BCT) instead of recess. The students loved that. When he left they all wrote sweet thank you letters. I liked the one written by a little girl. She said Mr. Gill had, "a nice loud vice." (Did she mean voice?)

Overcrowding may have contributed to Mark's discipline prob-lems, but he liked breaking rules. Sisters took turns phoning me about his peccadilloes and I would have to get the car from Bill, pack up the little ones, and drive about six miles to Hopewell to get him because the nuns punished him by not allowing him to ride the bus.

Not to be outdone, Michael got my attention after he was con-victed of "vandalism" and required to give Sister half his ten cent weekly allowance to repair damage to his desk. Bill began com-ing home after work, unlacing his boots, and paying Michael five cents to rub his aching feet so Michael would have money to pay the teacher. He also advised him against ever again being stupid enough to carve his own name in a desk.

Each day in "Kitchengarten" I strived to prepare Linda and the twins for first grade by teaching colors, numbers, letters, and how to follow instructions. Our kids all had chickenpox and Bill broke his left arm playing softball. I began to understand Miss Sack's advice about patience and decided God accepted prayers from harried moms even if their hands were submerged in a dishpan full of suds or busy cleaning and cooking all the time, like me.

And days passed into weeks and months. The children made a few friends and I thought Bill was happy at work. As it turned out we were in the shoals drifting before a perfect storm. Choppy wavelets should have warned of what was to come, but I ignored them until a Cuban named Fidel blew in like a typhoon and almost swamped us.

But, first things first. On a warm afternoon I was in the yard picking roses when a sergeant walked across the parking area, introduced himself as John A. He said he was a cook in the NONCOM Mess Hall. In my opinion he looked like the big, ugly, bruiser who stalked Popeye's girlfriend, Olive Oyle, but I didn't say that. From what he said next I guess he must have noticed that I recoiled.

"I'm originally from Dee-troit City and I know I look scary. Where I come from if they don't like your looks, they rearrange them. Don't be frightened. I just want to say hello."

A few minutes later I also met Melvie, the lady next door, whose Air Force husband was a sergeant stationed nearby at Washington Area Air Defense Sector (WAADS). In the months to come John and Melvie would play significant roles in my life, as would Joe, a member of the Army band who lived directly behind our quarters.

Fidel Castro caused all of us a problem that year, but so did the post commander.

A leaflet from the post commander's office was distributed to all quarters advising us about female deportment and dress codes. Female dependents older than twelve couldn't leave their quarters attired in shorts, not even to take kids to the playground. I wasn't going to obey an order I knew was stupid and probably illegal. To avoid a lecture on why I had to obey whatever the commanding general decreed I didn't share my opinion or my plan with Bill.

One friend and neighbor had five small children. Another had seven. The recent addition of John Franklin Gill born June twenty-second at Kenner Army Hospital brought the combined total of little kids under the age of ten to eighteen.

By zero nine hundred it was already ninety-five degrees Fahrenheit and we three petite young mothers donned shorts, pulled our hair into ponytails, and prepared to test the "no shorts rule." I herded the menagerie down the street with John sleeping in our German perambulator and all of us keeping an eye out for an MP patrol jeep, and giggling at the prospect of being taken into custody. Maybe, if we were lucky, to air conditioned solitary confinement? What would the MP do with the kids? We didn't care. Maybe the general would babysit while we were in the hoosegow.

Civil disobedience is every American's basic right. That's what our husbands went to war to protect. We didn't quite understand civil disobedience and were unaware we were jeopardizing our husbands' careers as we blithely marched toward Battlefield Park.

"Take us away," Mary said. "No, take the kids away." We laughed and agreed.

A Housing Area MP jeep driven by an ogling young soldier cruised by slowly and stopped. He made a show of counting heads before he spoke.

"It's a scorcher, isn't it? Where you ladies headed?"

"Right there. Battlefield Park," I thumbed toward the park. *Please take us away.*

Apparently that MP didn't care that we were blatant lawbreakers.

"Have fun," he said grinning as he sped away.

None of our husbands heard about our little excursion and we didn't repeat it. After that I gave up the idea of civil disobedience.

But then there was the thing about wearing socks in the PX. Fort Lee's new rule was simple. No socks, no admittance.

Late one Saturday afternoon Bill decided to run into the PX for some small item while I waited in the car with the kids. He parked, ran to the door and was stopped in his tracks.

"Halt," said the guard. "You can't enter, sir."

"Don't call me sir, corporal."

"Yes, sir. I mean no, sergeant. But you still can't come in. Not without socks."

"Are you kidding! Here's my ID. I'm wearing sandals and civvies. Don't need socks." He tried again to open the door and again was stopped.

"Orders, sergeant. Posted on the door. Can't let you in. Sorry, Sergeant Gill."

How would my *RA all the way* husband react?   He bit back his words and obeyed.

The GYN doctor had prescribed Valium, and I had a full bottle in my purse. I shook a pill into the palm of my hand and offered it to Bill, but he declined. He said it reminded him of the day back in South Carolina when "Nobody" ate the neighbor's hormone pills and I couldn't make them barf. He was right, of course, I tried but couldn't, but he still believed I shouldn't have called him home from work for such a minor problem.

CHAPTER 22

— ✂ —

Crisis is My Middle Name

IT HAPPENED ONE morning about zero nine hundred hours.

Linda slept in her buggy in the neighbor's kitchen while we three mothers gossiped. Mark, Michael, Billy One and Billy Two played in a bedroom. It became suspiciously quiet alerting Billy Number One's mother to check on them. She left Jennie and me drinking coffee in the kitchen while she walked down the hall to her son's room. A minute later we heard screams and ran toward the sound. She was ashen and looked ready to faint. In her hand she held an empty estrogen replacement pill bottle.

"That bottle had been full!" she said. "What happened to all the pills?"

We questioned each boy. I suspected four-year-old Mark of being the ring leader because of the smirk on his face, but he said nobody ate the pills. Did one child eat them all, or did they share? They all looked guilty. I asked Mark again, but his big, blue eyes stared back at mine. He smiled at me and continued to deny knowing anything. The other mothers quizzed each boy. The boys all agreed that nobody ate the pills.

While Billy One's mother telephoned the pharmacist for advice I tried unsuccessfully to gag the boys and make them throw up. I used a warm soapy solution. The boys began bawling and I felt like crying, too. I was scared. What harm would female hormones do to little boys?

Jennie said she had no idea, but it probably wouldn't be good.

We couldn't take the boys to the dispensary because none of us had a car and public transportation was nonexistent. Bill was an experienced medic. He'd know what to do. In desperation I phoned him at work, explained, and asked him to come home. He came at once, lined the boys in a row, ordered them to open their mouths, ran a finger down each throat, got the desired result, turned on his heel, and strode back toward the car.

I heard him grumble, "I've got to go to work."

Now, years later in front of the PX in Virginia, I had accidentally reminded him of that day. Again he said I should have been able to take care of *that* situation without involving him.

I couldn't help being unable to make little kids puke, Mister Smarty pants, but you should have read the general's notice letting you know about the no socks rule in the PX.

I wiggled my fingers in my ears and stuck out my tongue behind his back.

A few days later it was another scorcher and the older boys were in the yard squealing in fun and spraying each other with the garden hose. I was putting away toys on the patio and watching the twins toddle in tandem after a Monarch butterfly. I decided the picnic table took up too much space and would be better if outside the twelve inch high picket fence surrounding the patio and on the grassy spot closer to the kitchen door. I tried shoving the table, but it wouldn't budge. I tried moving one of the benches but they were bolted to the table.

The three older kids liked to eat outdoors. We'd picnic today. It wasn't a holiday, but it felt like one. I returned to the kitchen to collect paper plates, napkins, catsup, and of course, hotdog rolls. Bill finished mowing and came inside for a glass of iced tea.

"Whew! It's hot as Hell out there. We're eating out? Okay. What can I do to help get things ready?"

"Would you be able to move the picnic table?"

I explained my reason. I knew that inserting the word *able* was crucial. Bill believed there was *nothing* he wasn't *able* to do.

"Sure, Babe. Anything you say. Where do you want it?"

"Over in the shade. Near the kitchen door, please. That will be perfect."

I heard him yell, "Hey, boys. Mark? Mike? Come help me move the picnic table."

We've all heard the fable about the Little Red Hen who wanted some help baking bread. One morning she asked everyone in the barnyard to help. They had eaten her homemade bread every day but never helped make it. One by one they gave excuses until finally she baked the bread alone. When it was time to eat they all gathered around the table, but the Little Red Hen said, "I made it all by myself and now, I'm going to eat it all by myself."

Master sergeants seldom ask twice. They expect action after the first request, or order. Bill Gill never even heard of The Little Red Hen. In fact, he didn't know any of the nursery stories like Red Riding Hood, Bre'r Rabbit, etc. I heard his repeated request for help. Surprised, I went to the glass patio doors to watch. I was confident the boys would at least *try* to help, but they had ignored him and continued playing with the garden hose. As I stood at the window watching I couldn't have predicted what happened next.

Bill wore his Saturday work uniform culled from the rag bag. The ever present tattered and torn good luck field cap (patrol cap) he'd worn in 1951 under his helmet in Korea was perched atop his head. It was a hot day, but he wore his favorite stained, gray sweatshirt with cut off, un-hemmed sleeves, grease and paint splattered khaki shorts, and grass stained sneakers—a totally different appearance from his daily spit and polish.

I heard him call the boys again. I wasn't able to hear what they answered, but it was an unacceptable explanation as to why they couldn't come. They were only seven and eight years old. Were they really needed?

Bill would never allow me to help do "a man's job," so I started outside to say never mind. Just as I opened the door he whipped off his shirt, flexed his muscles twice and shouted, "Then, I'll do it myself!" Those words were followed by phrases favored by drunken sailors.

Bill was strong as a horse and stubborn as a bull. He hoisted the table above and over the picket fence, and dragged it to the spot I had indicated before he tripped on something—probably a toy of some kind—and fell.

I thought: *ten thousand souls arise; this isn't good.*And then I understood. Bill had needed the boys to be his eyes and direct him. I hurried outside to see if he was hurt.

He said he was fine but no longer in a mood to grill hotdogs. His version of *The Little Red Hen*? We ate in the kitchen and didn't mention the picnic table. But somebody had made an 8mm movie of it and we have watched him do it over, and over.

Following the picnic table event a ruthless young Fidel Castro began rattling his saber in Cuba and the arms race accelerated. By July the grapevine was flooded with news about Cuba and Fort Lee buzzed with unconfirmed reports. Everyone on the post, and WAADS, was on red alert.

Much of the scuttlebutt (gossip) centered on Cuba's ally, Communist Russia, and the missile launch photographed by our own spy planes only ninety miles from our coast in Mariel, Cuba. Our warships searched for Russian ships reportedly delivering nuclear warheads and if they discovered Russian submarines they dropped depth charges.

Hush-hush meetings of the brass produced myriads of rumors that kept changing. We believed we sat on a powder keg that would blow into World War III if somebody ignited it. Would it be President John Kennedy? We prayed he'd negotiate.

John Gill was four months old and small enough to sleep in a laundry basket, if necessary. I put blankets in a rectangular basket, just in case. Linda celebrated her fifth birthday with a party, but Castro made it a gut wrenching month for all of us. I told the children it was a hiding game and we played hiding in the front hall closet and then it was Black Saturday, October 17, 1962.

Jeeps with bitch boxes (public address system loud speakers) drove up and down the streets blaring warning announcements. Troops left for undisclosed coastal destinations. We dependents were reminded that our air raid shelters were the downstairs windowless closet of our quarters and were advised to store food and water there. It wasn't much protection from a nuclear blast. I knew there'd be few survivors and secretly perceived the front hall closet as a tomb where some future anthropologist might find our skeletal remains and wonder what happened.

What did Nikita Khrushchev want? He demanded The USA get our missiles out of Turkey. Would President Kennedy acquiesce? If not, was war coming to our shores?

I had grown accustomed to the Army policy of hurry up and wait. Like a good Army wife I'd immediately poured tap water into jars and put it, enough food for a few days, and necessities for "Baby John" in the closet, We began to wait—for what I wasn't sure.

One day our neighbor, the Mess Hall sergeant, pounded on our door and asked two questions: "You go to church, right?"

"Yes, John."

"If we go to war I don't want my kids to go to Hell. Will you baptize my kids?"

I said, "No." I could do so in dire circumstances, but I didn't think the situation quite warranted it.

I said, "I can set it up for you."

Bill and I took John's children to the chapel. An agitated colonel arrived before we finished and interrupted what we were doing.

"Put your name on a list," he told Bill. "Send half of all dental personnel to Florida. Do it right now. Let Mrs. Gill take care of the two kids." He left hurriedly. So did we.

Ground pounding grunts (infantry) began sharing fox holes with dental technicians and chaplain's assistants on Florida's beaches. I suspected having support troops in fox holes indicated extreme combat readiness.

"WAADS is on alert, too. We might actually have to fight the Commies this time, Babe. Castro's army has been shooting at American planes. I heard the sonofabitch wants Russia to nuke us."

"There's nothing I can do, so I'm going to act like this isn't happening," I said.

We lived on the edge, walked on eggshells, worried, and prayed. Then, as suddenly as it began it was over. War had been averted. Fort Lee's troops came home from Florida, our situation returned to SNAFU-- situation normal all f'd up-- or what usually passes in military life for normalcy and started preparing for the next crisis.

CHAPTER 23

———— ✂ ————

Flight # 374

I RETURNED EMERGENCY food to the kitchen, removed the laundry basket from the closet, and decided the water I'd bottled in every available container should probably be discarded. I carried several jugs out back to empty. Joe, a saxophonist originally from Cleveland, Ohio was a sergeant in the Army Band. He stood in his yard where ours and his joined before they both sloped down to a tiny free flowing creek.

"What are you doing, Joe?" I said grinning and pouring water on the thirsty grass.

"Same as you. I guess it's safe now. Mary has been real upset. She went through this kind of hell in Lebanon and it makes her sick on her stomach. How you doing?"

"I'm okay. I hate this whole thing, Joe. Not sure it's really over. What do you think?"

Joe shrugged. "They issued atropine to us, you know. In case the Russkies really nuke us. Just one dose! Who do I give it to? Colonel said I jab it in my own leg so I can fight. I wondered: should I give it to Mary or, maybe to one of our girls? How could they survive without me? What would I be fighting for?"

"Yeah. Terrible choice. I thought atropine was for muscle spasms, not nukes."

"Yeah, I think so, too. Who knows? Let's change the subject. Where's Bill today?"

"There was a bad plane crash. Bill and some of the others from the clinic had to go identify bodies by their dental records."

"Geeze. Well, I'm going to toot my horn a while. Good seeing you. I hope it's over."

When Bill came home he said he felt sick. I didn't mention my conversation about atropine. I could see he was already upset.

"The stench was terrible, Babe. Can't even describe it, but I don't think I'll ever eat pork chops again. That's kinda how it smelled. Like burned chops."

Gus, the sergeant holding the newly created rank of E-8 had been assigned to the clinic with the understanding he would be in charge of all enlisted personnel, including Bill who had been E-7 and Top Dog, a term of endearment referring to the fact that GI soldiers wore dog tags. This was a difficult adjustment for Bill who for ten years had held the highest rank. Now Gus would be the highest ranking enlisted soldier and be nicknamed Top Dog. Gus was a good soldier with a good reputation who hailed from Grand Isle and was a few years older than Bill.

"Gus is okay, Babe. I guess I actually like him as a person, but I sure do hate *this* situation. I want to be an E-8," he said. "That will require advanced classes at Brooke. Guess I'll put in a 1049, or something. I can't stand this much longer."

He seemed depressed about being outranked by Gus. I began to understand the importance of rank but had no idea what to do. A few days later Bill whistled up the sidewalk to the kitchen door, flung it open, grabbed me in his arms, and two-stepped us around the kitchen singing, "I'm going to Texas!" at the top of his voice.

"What! Why? When? For how long?"

"I told you. School. Advanced Dental Technician training. It's a TDY—a temporary duty—you won't have to move or anything, Babe. I'll be back in only sixteen weeks."

He just returned from Korea. This was proof of a secret pact with The Pentagon.

Bill was a happy camper while he was in Texas. The first time he was there, before he volunteered for Korea in 1950, he played football to keep fit. This time he'd acquire a deep tan from playing tennis and would also earn the certificate he wanted.

During his absence I played a lot of Scrabble with our next door neighbor, Melvie. When my paternal Grandmother Anderson unexpectedly died in her sleep I knew I had to go to Erie. Daddy had been close to his mother and needed me. I was hopeful I could find Erie by myself. The morning I got the news Melvie helped bundle the kids into our car and we headed north on a warm, spring morning.

My Swedish relatives lived in Jamestown, New York a short drive from Erie. As we crossed the New York line a state police car stopped us. The station wagon carried South Carolina tags, I had a Pennsylvania license, and the car was "garaged" in Virginia. I rolled down the window anticipating trouble.

"License and registration."

I handed them over. He didn't look at them. He motioned for his buddy to join us. He looked grim, like he expected, I couldn't guess. "Back seat," said the first officer.

The twins smiled from matching car seats equipped with little steering wheels.

"Those two?" He thumbed toward the twins. "They got licenses to drive?"

"No. They're only learning to be back seat drivers. Do they need a license for that?"

"Not in New York State. Where are you going?" he said with a grin handing back my license and registration. The other officer was smiling now, too.

"We're headed to Jamestown. To my grandmother's funeral."

"Oh. Sorry for your loss. Well, enjoy your visit to New York and drive safely."

I was right about my father. His grief was palpable. I held his hand and stood beside him at the open grave. To keep from bawling I mentally repeated the entire story of The Three Pigs, but backwards. I feared Daddy would fall into the pit, but afterwards he became himself again.

Three of my grandparents were dead. Only Grandpa Fabian was left. I decided to stay in Erie two weeks to let the kids enjoy *their* grandparents while they could.

We had barely arrived home in Virginia when Bill called and wanted to know why I hadn't been answering the phone. You must remember everything I'm telling you occurred before the invention of cell phones, personal computers, birth control, Homeland Security and airport security check points. Bill and I had been incommunicado while I was in Pennsylvania.

I told him I'd been "TDY" in Erie and he could have called there, if he'd been worried.

"Did you look for us? If you had tried, you could have found me, like in New Jersey!"

"Okay, Babe. You win. Let's not fight. Meet me at National Airport in D.C. We'll go see Paul and Marion and plan a beach vacation with them and the kids with the dough I'm saving on the price of air fare. I'm grabbing a hop on cargo flight #374. Be there at sixteen hundred."

I drove to D.C. and arrived punctually, but he wasn't there. After waiting an hour I spoke with a desk clerk, told him my husband was arriving from Texas on flight #374, and asked him to check the passenger manifesto.

"I'm concerned," I said. "He's not usually late like this. When will he arrive?"

"Guys do it all the time. Go home, Miss. He's not coming. There's no flight #374."

I called Marion's husband, Paul. He said, "Sit tight. I'll deal with that guy for you."

Paul tried but the clerk was adamant that no flight #374 existed. I told Paul to go back home. I said I'd sit there until Bill arrived. As day became evening I worried about plane crashes and mentally bit my fingernails. Finally, I moved outside to wait in our car.

Passengers arrived and left in a steady stream, but I didn't see anyone looking like my husband. I did notice a man with a military buzz, aviator shades, and dark skin wearing a maroon jacket. He looked like a New Orleans jazz musician. I was stunned. Was he waving at me? How dare he! I certainly didn't wave back, but I looked more closely.

He was still frantically waving in my direction. I looked behind but seeing nobody there I squinted and looked at the fresh guy again. This time I had a new thought. I drove very slowly to where he stood, pulled up beside him, and stopped.

"Want a ride, soldier?" I said laughing.

Bill had such a dark tan I hadn't recognized him. I thought that was funny. The past months had been difficult and we both needed a break and a good laugh, but it was going to get much more difficult. Worse than Fidel Castro's threats, or grandma's death, crowded schools, separations? Yes. Life with a soldier suffering from itchy feet and a desire for a promotion is a teeter totter ride that won't stop or let you get off.

That year Bill had three dissimilar experiences with airplanes. One, of course, was when he hopped from Texas and was delayed because the pilot went from Texas to Virginia via Kansas and St. Louis. The second was the downed Army plane when he helped ID passengers who were burned beyond recognition. About the same time one of Bill's friends boarded a "Flying Tiger" headed

145

to Japan. They took off from California and disappeared over the Pacific. No wreckage was found. These things bothered him, but something else bothered him more than all those events combined. His friendly smile became a nasty grumble. He became a grouch.

"I hate having an E-8 over me, Babe. Gus is okay, but...I've got somebody at the Pentagon looking out for me so I can get E-8. There might be an opening in St. Looey. Whatchasay?"

Proof of conspiracy? "I guess that means moving to St. Louis, Missouri? When?"

"That's my girl. Hey! Scoot over my lap. I'll drive. It's too hard for you."

I scooted and told myself I didn't want to drive in D.C. traffic anyway. *Yeah, too hard except when you leave us here or want me to pick you up at the airport!*

"Did you miss the kids? They aren't with me."

"Yeah, where are the little rug rats?"

"Patricia is keeping them for us."

"I like that idea. Shall we pull off somewhere, get naked, and reacquainted?"

One thing about being a military spouse, although it's intense at times and filled with stressful events, if you can figure out how to adapt to a crisis every time you turn around it can be wonderful. If you find a soldier who is sober, steady and loyal—not easy to do, but if you do find that rare soldier and marry him, you won't ever be bored.

CHAPTER 24

— ❧ —

1963

BILL HOPED TO receive orders to anywhere that wasn't Fort Lee. He didn't get a PCS (permanent change of station) to St. Louis. He tried to arrange an overseas assignment and convinced the PIO (public information officer) to take a new passport photo for us.

"Let's be ready," he said, "in case I get orders and we get the H… out of Fort Lee."

There were no overseas orders, but I did get a nice group photo of the kids and me. And we all got caught up on our immunizations. Especially, Robert.

After waiting in a long, slow line until I was ready to walk out of the dispensary it was our turn. I herded all the kids into a room where a nurse waited and told her we needed to update everyone's shot record. She administered a green glob of smallpox vaccine on Robert's arm before turning away a nanosecond. While she wasn't watching him, and I wasn't quick enough, he ran his index finger across the site, scooped up the vaccine and promptly ate it. He looked up at me with a big grin. He'd eaten his small pox vaccine! What would it do to him? I was scared. I tried to keep an eye on the others, but my main focus stayed on Robert. Mark, Michael and Linda were old enough to know how to wait.

"Look!" I was in panic mode. "He ate the green stuff! What will happen to him?"

"Not much. He just vaccinated himself inside out." She was an experienced nurse.

We spent the next several minutes getting injections in arms and butts until finally we were done. I gathered up our things, including John's stuffed Mousie, and prepared to leave. "Are we all done?"

"Yes, Mrs. Gill. You're ready to go overseas. Don't worry about the boy."

As summer faded into autumn we still waited and hoped. Then it was time for school again. Bill was depressed. He wanted to buy a new car. One day I said it suited me and would give him something to take his mind off getting orders. He bought a brand new green VW bus with an aisle to walk from the front to the rear. I hated it on sight and said Hiss! Boo! After that, the VW was always referred to as the "Boo" bus.

Bill loved that monster vehicle with its windows and rows of seats. I was glad he had the diversion because we lingered in limbo land until nearly Halloween when orders finally arrived. Bill would be an E-8 at Fifth Army Headquarters in Hyde Park, Chicago.

The third week of November in 1963 we piled into the VW and headed there via Erie. You guessed it. We had to drive our green VW through a cold, nasty snowstorm and we wouldn't get to Chicago that day, or the next. First, we would be forced to experience a national disaster and the threat of imminent war. Bill would arrive alone in the Windy City and the kids and I would spend an extended visit in Erie.

We left the sunshine in Virginia and by the time we neared Breezewood and were ready to approach the on ramp to the Pennsylvania Turnpike Indian summer weather had vanished. Cold gusts whipped fresh snow across the highway dangerously rocking our VW bus. The sky was gunmetal gray and dull. But it wasn't that that got my full attention. It was seeing uniformed men standing along the road beside sea bags and duffle bags. It was eerie like a scene from a Hitchcock movie. I wondered why they were there. It felt ominous. We both knew soldiers don't stand outdoors in the cold without a very good reason.

We pulled in at a gas station/restaurant just before the Turnpike and Bill went inside to ask what had happened. Although it looked treacherous to even walk in the storm, when he returned he was running, and he wasn't smiling, It was bad news.

"Everybody and his brother are inside with their eyes glued to the television."

"What is it? What's happened?" He handed me a paper cup of hot coffee.

"Kennedy's been shot. Probably the Commies are at it. Nobody knows who did it."

"Is he going to live?" We skidded out of the parking lot and headed north.

"Maybe. No, probably not. I've got to report in somewhere. I'm not sure where."

"Are we at war? I mean, our president has been shot. Won't that start a war?"

"Maybe. If he dies. They took him to the hospital. Nobody knows his condition."

"What are we going to do? What about the children?"

"I'll go on to Chicago and report in. I'll leave y'all with your folks. Don't' worry. Soon as possible I'll come for you."

"No. I want to come with you. I don't want to be dropped off in Pennsylvania. If you go to Chicago, so am I. We'll leave the kids with my mother."

"No. You are not. You're staying with your folks. I'm going to Chicago. When it's safe, I'll come and get you. Y'all aren't going with me. Period. No way, Jose. Forget it."

When we arrived in Erie Daddy was watching TV. President Kennedy was dead. Vice-president Johnson had been sworn in as president. We watched a terrified First Lady wearing a blood smeared pink outfit crawl over the back of an open convertible again and again until the familiar peacock logo signaled the television station was off the air until the next day.

Mother was a staunch Republican but Daddy loved and always supported Kennedy. He was convinced the murder bore "the fingerprint of the Russkies." Everyone blamed Lee Harvey Oswald, but we would never know for sure who really killed President John Fitzgerald Kennedy.

The kids and I remained in Erie three weeks before Bill returned and we piled in the VW for the long drive to Chicago. Snow chased us all the way from Erie and by the time we parked in front of our new home in Southside Chicago we were tired and hungry but to get to the house from the street we had to scale mounds of dirty snow.

By flickering street lights I saw we were in a poor, urban neighborhood *under* the overpass we'd just traveled on. Our house was a new three bedroom brick ranch style, but most of the neighboring buildings were World War I two story frame structures. We had a large back yard adjacent to a prairie and railroad tracks. The full basement was finished with wood paneling. Our quarters were great, but why were we living in Southside? Why not north of Chicago, or at Fort Sheridan?

I didn't understand what was at play, but something didn't feel right. I didn't voice any negative thought and pretended it was perfect because that's what Army wives do. We make do and try not to complain, but I felt something was happening that I didn't understand. I tried to set aside my concerns and began adapting to our neighborhood.

We enrolled the children in a parochial elementary school a block away. When I asked a nun why the police officer was in the hall she said, "The cops patrol halls to keep down on the number of rapes occurring in school." It was a school for little kids! We had sent ours there, instead of to the reportedly dangerous public schools, believing they'd be safer.

One cold and sunny day after we had been there about a week Michael fell in the school yard severely cutting his leg. A car full of strangers pulled into our driveway leaving the motor running. Our phone rang as a strange young man in a dark suit dashed from the car to our door. I answered the phone and heard, "Father is on his way."

"There's been an accident," the man in black said identifying himself as the parish priest. "Eighth grade girls will babysit your little ones. Michael's in the car. Let's go."

I quickly dialed the Butterfield Eight phone number at Fifth Army Headquarters. "Bill!" I yelled when he answered, "Meet me at the hospital." I hung up, grabbed my purse and ran out to the car where I found Michael stretched out in the back seat with red blood oozing from a large gash. He apologized for tearing his school pants. I said, "Don't worry." We went to the nearest hospital because I had no idea what to do or where to go.

"We're going to have to remove his leg," a white coated doctor said. I objected and the priest asked what else they could do. "Cheaper to do that," the doctor said. I protested again.

Somebody holding a pencil poised over a clipboard said in an unmistakable *don't mess with me* voice, "What's your address?"

"I don't remember. We're new here. Maybe this priest might know?"

She wrote down that he guessed it was ninety-six hundred South Houston Avenue.

"Telephone?"

"It's unlisted. I don't remember the number."

"Do you have cash to pay for this visit, Mrs. Gill?" asked clipboard lady.

"I don't carry cash." I didn't cry. I was still so shocked I couldn't even think.

"Can you get some?" the priest interjected. He had seen where this was going.

"Cash? No. I doubt it. I don't know. What for? Why? How much?"

He asked the woman who drove us to the hospital to return to the school and get some cash for me.

"Oh," I said. "Thank you, but she doesn't need to do that. We don't need money."

"I thought you said you don't have insurance or any cash," clipboard lady said.

"I don't. The Army will pay. For everything. Please, if it's possible, save his leg."

Once the doctor knew the Army would pay the hospital charges he decided amputation wasn't required and began the process to save Michael's leg while I tried to make sense of what was happening. I did realize the priest was concerned about liability issues and made a mental note to tell him not to worry.

That night I grilled Bill about why he hadn't joined me at the hospital. "I needed you!"

"I tried, Babe. I waited for you to call, but you didn't. Do you have any idea how many hospitals are in Chicago? You didn't say which one, so I didn't know where to go."

That introduction to Chicago set the pace. We lived there while black terrorists tried to burn the city down, and white neighbors assured me they'd kill any black person who dared step on our street.

152

At the same time the same people would stop me and the kids wherever we happened to be, make the sign of the cross and say, "Oh, God bless you, five sons, and a princess!"

Linda liked being a seven-year-old princess. She also liked to sing and she was positive her daddy was important enough to pick up our phone and call somebody to arrange an audition for the Ed Sullivan Show. All that year she begged Bill to get her on television. She wanted to perform "The Old Family Toothbrush," a parody sung to the tune of "The Old Oaken Bucket." She begged and begged, but to no avail. Linda's disappointment lasted years.

An Italian neighbor taught me how to make pizza. Another one, an elderly widow, had missed the sailing of the Titanic. Others had escaped from Communist Yugoslavia and President Tito. Many of these first generation Americans were church goers, but they readily admitted they hated all blacks, Mexicans, most Serbs, or Croats—former Yugoslavians, several other groups, and some-times, each other.

Didn't they get it? America is the land of the free and the home of the brave. Isn't that why they came? Everybody here is equal. I tried, but couldn't understand them. I also tried being a peace-maker in Southside Chicago in the 1960s. Who was I kidding?

I asked a neighbor if she'd prefer a nice, educated, Christian, *black* family living next door to her, or poor, ignorant, drunk, wife beating, *white* trash. The point I was making blew up in my face when she didn't choose the nice black family.

"I'll take white trash," she said, chin jutting, hands on hips, dar-ing me to disagree.

Chicago is composed of many small communities where every-one knows who is an outsider and who belongs. It was those tightly knit boundaries that had been breached by activists. It was those people, in those communities, that our leaders hoped to peacefully

integrate. And it was those same people who were just as determined that it wasn't happening without "blood in the street."

Were we some kind of soft blockbusters, an acceptable white
Army family, sent there to lull the neighbors into complacency? I
hoped that wasn't true, but it was one theory of how a neighborhood organizer might try to integrate a Chicago neighborhood.
Would it work? Probably not.

CHAPTER 25

— ⚭ —

Footlockers

BILL WAS A handsome hero with a charming personality. Everyone was his new friend. Ergo! Acceptable. The Gills were a Donna Reed family and we were invited to functions, into homes and treated with kindness and respect. Our innocent neighbors thought it was fine to have Army families (like us) among them. What they didn't realize was the next Army family might not be white, might not have children, and might be unfriendly, but it would be too late—the neighbors had already agreed to having military families live in their community.

For two years we did touristy things like going to the beach, visiting museums, St. Patrick's Day parades, and shopping. Chicago's a wonderful town, but you must have money to enjoy it. It's expensive anywhere with six children. On Army pay Chicago was very expensive and our budget was stretched to the breaking point.

Bill took a night job at the A&P and was required to join a union. "I can't do that," he said. When he was told to join or don't work, he joined. He worked at Fifth Army Headquarters by day and stocked shelves at A&P in South Chicago until midnight.

Mark's teacher asked him to tell his school class what his father did for a living. Mark was obsessed with money, status, position, etc. and longed to be a millionaire. He said, "My father works in stocks." We will never know whether it was a conscious effort to make Bill sound prosperous or only an innocent error to ignore that Bill was in the Army, but it gave me lots of chuckles. Still

The A&P discarded a sinful amount of food. Late at night when his shift at the store was ending one of Bill's tasks was to throw all bread products in the dumpster because, according to the manager, day-old products were unfit to sell. Bill asked if he could bring it home instead of throwing it away and was granted permission. I didn't have to buy bread products for a long time and we ate donuts, cake, pie and all types of bread until we got sick of it.

"I could try to get a job," I offered. "Do something to help with expenses."

"You have a job right here. I'll earn the money. Just tell me how much you need."

In a few months Bill itched to be promoted to E-9, another new rank. He said we needed the pay increase that came with the rank of sergeant major. It meant moving.

"There's an opening in Germany. Let's go back to Germany. Whatchasay, Babe?"

"Why not? Sure. We've already had overseas shots and a passport photo. Go for it."

Our neighbors gave us a wonderful going away party. With mixed emotions we left Illinois toward the end of 1965 to return to the suburban township where my parents lived. I rented a house, enrolled the kids in school, and we lived in Pennsylvania a few months while Bill went to Germany to get promoted and accept housing in Schwabisch Hall, a German town close to France and The Czech Republic.

The holidays were spent with my family, the children made friends in school, and time passed. When Bill said he was ready and waiting for us I knew to expect a port call and began preparations by installing a blackboard in the kitchen like a menu board except instead of listing food it listed German vocabulary words. I wanted to immerse the children in the German language before moving there.

Only days before our departure I noticed John needed an additional overseas shot. There wasn't an Army installation within a hundred miles. What did civilians do? They didn't have to go overseas. Did civilians get immunizations? Where was the nearest military facility? I didn't know what to do. I did know I had to get John vaccinated. Somebody, I think my friend and neighbor during high school, Jimmy Mason, told me about a Marine Corps clinic in downtown Erie near Tenth Street.

I phoned and got an appointment at the small clinic which fortunately for us was staffed by a Marine medic with a heart of gold. He was a blessing because John Franklin Gill had made up his mind to not be vaccinated, and since he was part hardheaded Swede, he was stubborn.

John was three and a half years old and still kept his favorite toy, a big floppy-eared gray mouse named Mousie, next to him at all times. At the clinic he refused to let go of it, or me, looking askance and openly suspicious of the big Marine. He absolutely refused to get a shot. But he absolutely had to!

"Hey, buddy! Can I see Mousie?" The Marine was trying to make friends, but John pulled back and tried to hide behind me. I nudged him. He had to have the shot.

"Will you stick out your arm for me, pal? It will only hurt a tiny minute. Okay?"

John shook his head.

"Aw, come on, pal. Just a little prick and we're all done."

"No!"

"If I give Mousie the first shot and he doesn't cry, will you?"

After being asked twice John reluctantly agreed. He watched like a hawk as the corpsman carefully injected Mousie. When Mousie didn't cry John smiled and stuck out his little arm. I thanked the Marine for his understanding and in two minutes we were ready to go.

Well, almost ready to go. We had a port call, we had our shots, we knew Bill had an apartment ready. We had plane tickets to Philadelphia. There was one more important thing to do and it was no small feat: I had to pack for all of us. Packing for six kids needing winter snowsuits, boots and mittens for a move to another country is not easy.

Each of us could take two suitcases. That's fourteen suitcases, or the equivalent. Mark was almost eleven years old—by Army standards still a child—and not very strong which meant the gigantic task was left to me. I knew we couldn't carry that many suitcases, not even if all the kids helped.

I started thinking outside the box, or in my case, outside the suitcase. With the help of Mother Necessity a nebulous idea began to grow and take shape. I don't remember exactly how it happened, but something inspired me and I remembered footlockers in the basement. I let the idea roll around and gel—it sounded crazy even to me—but it was crazier to think I could carry fourteen suitcases!

The idea took on a life of its own. I finished fixing lunch and began to sort things into piles to ship, take, toss, or store. In the back of my mind I thought about footlockers.

CHAPTER 26

—— ✑ ——

Meeting Doctor Fool

Some diehards denied Germany unconditionally surrendered in 1945 following her defeat in World War II, but they couldn't deny The Allies divided Germany into sectors for Great Britain, France and the United States leaving Berlin to communism and the Russians. East Germany under the Russians hadn't moved forward, but other sectors had changed. Seated on the sofa thinking about suitcases and the Germany we left ten years ago, and wondering if any significant changes had taken place, I recalled that Eisenhower had been president then.

Although I hadn't voted for "Ike" because I was too young to vote, and I hadn't truly understood its historical importance, I was sorry I followed Bill's request to stay home instead of going downtown to participate in the inaugural activities in 1953. We didn't know it then, but I had already begun turning into the history buff I became and would have a front row seat at a few historical events, but not Eisenhower's celebration.

I thought way back to the summer I turned twelve. After we heard the news on August 14th we ran outside and banged pots and pans in the backyard to celebrate Victory in Japan (V-J Day) with our neighbors. Mother said everyone did the same on Armistice Day, November 11th in 1918 when she was fifteen and World War I ended.

Americans thought 1945 marked the end of the war, but in Germany it was the end of the "Thousand Year Reich" and the

beginning of year zero. For Germans 1945 was also a time of starvation, fuel shortages, housing shortages, and freezing cold tem-
peratures when everyone had to forage for food, begging a cup
of milk by the teaspoonful and bartering for necessities as paper
money became worthless.

It was not uncommon for a woman to exchange a solid gold
bracelet for a pound of butter. Year Zero was a time of limbo—a
time when humanness was reduced to its lowest level. German
citizens had to start all over from nothing. Cheating, stealing, lying,
all manner of criminal activity and especially black marketing ran
amuck. For women—young and old—whoring became a way of
life that provided very little in material wealth. Men with money who
bought their services referred to the females as meat. Those men,
often soldiers, were expected to give a chocolate bar, some soap,
a small morsel of food, or a pair of nylons in exchange for sex—
and the women were willing to trade in order to stay alive. But sex
customers often reneged when the time to pay came. And many
women were impregnated by men they never saw again. Only the
fittest survived. Only the lucky escaped. Some of the lucky ones
emigrated to America.

Germans who were children in 1945 have grown old. Soon
there will be no one left to remind the world of the millions who
died *after* the end of the war, during the time known as Year
Zero. Possibly it is a time best forgotten—and many have forgotten already-- but if we do forget, if nations forget, historians
assure us that we are bound to repeat everything that led up to
the nothingness.

By the time I first arrived in Germany in January of 1954 the situation had improved. A little. Life was still difficult, but a sense of
normalcy prevailed. German civilians—there was no German military—tried to adapt. Some hated Americans and made no secret

of it, but most at least pretended to like us, or at the very least tried to get along with us, and create new lives. In 1955 a big occasion was scheduled.

I had missed Eisenhower's inauguration but in 1955 Bill invited me to attend a ceremony marking the end of ten years of American occupation and rule in Ulm/New Ulm, and all of Germany. I was thrilled I'd witness a ceremony to return sovereignty to Germans allowing them to build a self-defense military and prosper. While suspicious, cautious, fearful nations watched I'd be a tiny speck observer of world changing history as it happened.

In 1955 American women living in Germany usually ordered clothes from catalogs like Sears & Roebuck because the European Exchanges sold few items for civilians. I wanted to look my best at the ceremony and make Bill proud. I wanted to wear an American made outfit and asked Mother to send something appropriate from The Boston Store. She had them ship a lightweight woolen suit that fit like it had been tailored for me and was the same shade of blue as my eyes.

On The Big Day we were greeted with cirrus clouds and gray skies. A chilly breeze turned leaves over—a prediction of rain. Braving a damp, unpredictable climate invited pneumonia or another bout with bronchitis. It was a dilemma. But I refused to cover up my new outfit with a coat or slicker. I prayed the weather would improve but while pondering possible options I remembered a dress hanging in the wardrobe and flung open the door. There it was—the answer to my problem-- a tight fitting long-sleeve silk-jersey dress. "Aha!" I said, yanking it off its hanger and slipping it over my head. It felt like a second skin and made me warm. I added a new white silk blouse with attached frilly lace jabot, slipped into the suit jacket, closed the snaps on the skirt, stepped into spectator pumps, and looked in a large mirror. The layered look worked perfectly.

The addition of a little rouge, blue eye shadow, and bright red lipstick completed a stylish image. Satisfied with my appearance I went to find Bill who gave a long, low wolf whistle when he saw me. I knew he might, but he also insisted I would look great wearing a burlap bag.

"You look gorgeous, Babe... a very sexy cross between Lauren Bacall and Doris Day."

※

It was a nice memory but I quit procrastinating, sighed and resumed the task of sorting things to ship to Germany from those like my piano that would be stored three years. I'd already given away household items, clothes, and toys in order to comply with weight restrictions imposed by the Army. When I began sorting books I realized we owned a lot of books. I started with Collier's encyclopedias, Webster's dictionary and dozens of Little Golden children's books setting aside Bill's as they were designated professional material and excluded from our household weight allowance. I was an eclectic reader liking everything from A to Z. Bill preferred The Wall Street Journal, Army Times, local newspapers, and anything that pertained to the Army, football or politics. But his favorite reading material was Army regulations, training manuals, and reports issued by the Government Printing Office (GPO). My favorites were adventure, mystery, history, religion, psychology and how-to books and I owned dozens of them.

My thoughts drifted back to 1956 in Germany and I wondered what would be familiar, and what had changed since we left there. I knew that in 1956 factories opened and gave employment to girls who had worked for Americans as maids and nannies. When two MPs came for our maid, Rosie, I couldn't believe my eyes and ears and phoned Bill.

"They want to take Rosie, right now. They said she's going to work in some factory beginning immediately. They won't even let her finish dong the ironing, Bill! What should I do?"

"Obey the MPs, Babe. Let Rosie go. She'll be fine."

"But I owe her wages and don't have any money."

"Tell her to meet her friend, Ginny. Give her pay to Ginny to give her later. You know Ginny, the one who works for your friend, Alice. And wish Rosie good luck."

I can't say how many girls left the same way. Maybe none. American military families were "encouraged"to hire maids to help the ecomony. Girls lucky enough to be employed by American families had short work weeks, a room of their own, food, and cash. The day Rosie left—I could almost say was rounded up and removed from our Housing Area against her will—to work in a factory to help jump start that business possibly helped her financially and socially, but it bothered me that she was forced to move from refugee, to maid, to factory employee status.

I ordered myself back to the task before me. I knew that I had to concentrate on the present and stop thinking about ten years ago. I had to solve a luggage problem for six children and myself and time was running out.

We owned a small set of brown leather luggage consisting of a cosmetic case, an overnight, and a train case—not nearly enough for seven people. I pictured us dressed in multiple layers, but that wouldn't work. Mail our clothing? I discarded that notion. Ship it in sacks or cardboard boxes? No. Buy all new in Germany? Too expensive. Then I had an inspiration.

Every GI family owns footlockers! Footlockers, so called because they sat at the foot of cots in barracks, had hinged lids and padlock hasps and could lock up all the worldly goods of one soldier. They are sturdy, wooden, rectangular, green crates big enough to hide two small children, two large quilts, or our clothing, teddy bears and other necessary items. We had accumulated a supply of lockers to use for toy boxes, storing linen, keeping tools, sewing, garden items, and more.

I ran to the cellar to count them and discovered seven perfectly good specimens complete with keys and padlocks! A bag for Band-Aides, snacks and little stuff like make-up, and a shoulder strap purse left a free hand to hold onto "Baby John." When we went to Philadelphia the seven green footlockers went, too.

At the airport I stepped forward when our name was called and tried to look demure. Six cherubic youngsters lined up behind me and stood patiently before a bored Army specialist who told me to put Gill luggage on a huge scale. His eyes didn't leave his clipboard until I said, "I can't." I pointed a gloved finger at seven footlockers neatly arranged behind six children.

I thought our use of footlockers was brilliant, and very much Army. Not everyone agreed—especially the Army specialist who weighed our luggage in Philadelphia and the men in Frankfurt who'd come in staff cars to transport our suitcases and saw seven matching green footlockers was our only luggage. I thanked everyone as nicely as possible but I knew they weren't happy about it and didn't share my enthusiasm for footlockers.

Nobody guessed I couldn't afford, or carry, fourteen suitcases and that was the reason we didn't travel like normal people. Nothing about Army life is normal, so what? If questioned, I said I did it because we are an Army family. Some people even believed me when I said, "We're RA all the way and If one of the Gills bleeds, we bleed olive drab instead of red."

Looking back I suspect my future rebellious behavior might have begun then. At first, it was little things, like the color of blood or odd luggage, but it escalated in 1968 when Russian tanks lined the border near our quarters in Erlangen. That's when I debated the Army's evacuation plans for dependents.

I was actually fed up with military life, disliked the way wives were treated as second class citizens and/or sex objects, frustrated, overstressed, and sick. Something had to change. I started by declaring the evacuation plans unworkable. I needed to convince others. And I longed to feel normal—whatever that was.

I wanted some permanency and a house where I could paint the walls any color I chose, stomp on the grass if I felt like it, build a fence, park a bike in the yard, leave dirty dishes in the sink. And, I wanted to live where I wouldn't hear the perpetual sound of tanks outside my window while I prayed they were *our* tanks.

Bill didn't notice how sick I was. When I told him his only advice was to go see the doctor at the Medical Clinic. I asked Bill to request a compassionate transfer back to the States so I could go to an internist but he wouldn't consider that. Why couldn't he see I wasn't okay? Did I need to die to get his attention?

I was burdened with responsibilities. I was the Cadet Girl Scout leader, helped with a cotillion for American young people, taught in the Sunday school and cared for our large family. Finally, I went to see the battalion Army doctor, a captain who would treat us as a professional courtesy and said he'd never allow members of our family to be treated by Doctor Steppenenko, a foreign national who barely spoke English.

I lost count of the mistakes he made that I personally witnessed, but Bill steadfastly refused to intervene because he doubted my assessment of the captain's ineptitude. Bill thought I overreacted when I listed my complaints.

Linda was treated medically, but actually required surgery that she eventually got once we returned to the States. The captain claimed Mark's bleeding *couldn't* be caused by mononucleosis because he was "too young." He changed his mind after lab results. Michael was already scheduled for nonelective surgery at Nurnberg, but couldn't go until the captain agreed, Robert was unconscious after a fall and received no treatment, John was unconscious after being hit by a neighbor's car but untreated, and Thomas—referred to as the puny one because he got sick easily-- wasn't helped. One at a time he ignored or misdiagnosed each of us. I began thinking of him as Doctor Fool and tried to see the foreign civilian, or a corpsman, but I was thwarted. A neighbor whose husband was in the medical battalion went to the clinic because she felt unwell. The captain insisted on providing her with professional courtesy, too. He misdiagnosed a pregnancy as a tumor and the fetus later died. That captain wasn't only a fool, he was a dangerous fool.

One afternoon I broached a new topic with Doctor Fool. "Well," I began, "if you can't find anything wrong with me how about send-ing me to a shrink? I *know* something's wrong. Is it mental? Maybe I'm imagining it? I don't know. Maybe I'm nuts."

"Okay," he agreed. But quickly added, "Remember, you asked for this...."

In 1968 it was unusual for a patient to willingly seek help from a psychiatrist. People declined to admit anything was wrong mental-ly. I didn't know it but soldiers often denied having posttraumatic stress (now referred to as PTSD) because of the negative stigma, or they sought help furtively. I did know it was possible for a psychoso-matic illness and/ or prolonged stress to cause physical problems. I wondered: If I thought myself sick, could I think myself well?

Before my appointment with the Army psychiatrist in Nurnberg Doctor Fool prescribed Thorazine, a strong medicine used to treat schizophrenia. I took it exactly as prescribed but it didn't make me feel better.

Bill drove me to the appointment in Nurnberg but refused to enter the old brick building even after I pleaded with him. I was afraid to go alone but he absolutely refused to go with me.

"I'm up for promotion. I can't be seen coming in a place like *that*. I'd never get promoted if they thought I need a head doctor. I'll wait here, in the parking area."

I climbed up old concrete steps repeating the words to a song: I Wanna Go Home. By the time I reached the top I was thinking: *O-oh, how I wanna go home,* and didn't mean to our quarters. My husband had deserted me. Again. And I wanted Daddy.

But first I had to know if I was crazy. It was easier than expected. The doctor read my health record, examined me, and asked questions. I told him the Thorazine had caused horrible nightmares and made me perspire profusely.

"If *you* don't think I am nuts, could I stop taking it? I hate the way it makes me feel. I only took it because my doctor said I had to."

"Don't take any more. Medicine is supposed to make you feel better, not worse."

"Thanks. Something is wrong with me. Is it psychosomatic? Am I making it up? What do you think? Am I crazy?"

"Would you like to see what I've written on your record?"

He turned the folder so I could see it. I read: there's nothing wrong with this patient, return her to medical. That was good news and bad news. A return to medical meant going back to Doctor Fool.

Consequentially, I continued to have strange symptoms and grew weaker. I felt cold all the time, and began to believe I would die. Captain Fool didn't understand hypothyroidism. Neither did I.

CHAPTER 27

Tanks for the Memory

RUSSIAN SOLDIERS AND tanks played psychological war games with The Czech Republic by rolling up to the German border near Prague to enforce communist rule. Russian tankers feigned surprise when they were told it was not a war game. Asked why they were doing it they claimed Czechs had become belligerent and had to be stopped from promoting propaganda against communism. By force, if required.

Holy Toledo! I was unprepared for this!

I remembered my Romanian friend, Nantchi. After she'd been a political prisoner she dreaded being recaptured by "Russian pigs" and returned to the gulag. I began feeling fear—gut wrenching physical fear for my children--for all of us. What were the Russians thinking? Did they plan to start another war? With the United States?

It was a yellow alert as American tanks rolled up and down in front of our apartment. We were under a threat of siege. Or, were we? *Was this a possible red herring? Was it merely a political ploy to keep Americans from noticing the Tet Offensive slaughter of American troops in 'Nam*?

International politics is a complicated business with strategies inside strategies, inside strategies, inside strategies, and nothing appearing as it really is-- like a Chinese puzzle or Russian stacking doll. We understood Russia wanted to keep The USA from making friends with China. But *what woke up "The Bear?"* Why were they lined up on the other side of the border looking toward Germany?

Russia had tried an entry level form of socialism in the 1940s moving steadily toward communism and ruthlessly converting willing and unwilling people. What were they up to now? Whatever it was, it made me nervous.

On a hot day in 1968 The Fourth Armored Division moved tanks into position and Russians maneuvered theirs lining up on both sides of the border. If Russians invaded they would take everything in sight, share it among the elite, let the proletariat starve, and slaughter dissidents, like me. Only our military would stand in their way.

Communists believed if you don't work, you don't eat, but jobs were scarce in Russia, food was difficult to get, and people went hungry. One thing I knew for certain: I didn't want Russians taking over and fervently prayed the punto murerto—the Spanish stand-off didn't escalate and the Russian soldiers went back home without a fight.

Maria, a middle-age putzfrau (cleaning lady) who worked in our building was concerned for my safety and told me to go home to New York, meaning anywhere in the United States.

"Go back to the land of the round door knobs, Mrs. Gill. You don't belong here.

Go home. It isn't safe for you if the Russians cross the border, who knows what the Americans would do, but it will be bad. You don't want to be in the middle."

"Can't do that. You survived World War II, Maria. Don't you know some place?"

I thought about hideaway places, bomb shelters, etc. She should know. She held her hands palms up, raised her eyebrows, and shrugged like a haggling fish monger.

"When Hitler came, we took off our Girl Scout uniforms and buried them. Hitler didn't like Girl Scouts. Afterwards, we dug them up again. Now? I'm Czech. Prague is my home. Where can I flee? But you? Ja? You should go home before it's too late."

"The Colonel asked if I want to but he hoped I wouldn't because if I left it would cause panic among the other wives and ruin morale. I asked him why I'd want to be in The States if Bill's not. If my husband is going to die over here, so am I. I *won't* leave."

"You should, but who knows? Maybe the Russians back down!"

"What have you read in the Nurnberg papers? Tell me what's in the paper. I can read a little, but not about things like this. My German isn't that good. Tell me what you read in the papers."

"Did you hear about the people standing at the border in a long line with arms locked? Men, women, children, and old people—maybe a few American, ja? They were there and called out to the Russians. 'Go home, brother.' But they stay. Because of orders they say, but whose orders? What are they planning? All those civilian people. they were brave, no?"

"I didn't know about that, but I heard about a young man, a boy, who was seen changing the street signs. He said he turned them around to confuse the enemy if they dared advance onto German soil. That was smart and brave, too."

"Ja! I pray they turn those tanks around and go home. I survived one war, that's true. But I don't want to do it again. Maybe the Russian dogs don't really want to start something with the United States, eh? Maybe they're just baring their fangs? Russia likes to do that. I've seen it before."

In case of an invasion American schools stayed closed to avoid potential problems.

As a result of my still undiagnosed Hashimoto Syndrome (hypothyroidism) I felt weaker with each passing day and wore sweaters in the apartment and a coat if I went out. When war appeared inevitable I used a Magic marker and printed Gill on the kids' clothes and Bill's RA number on their backs like a tattoo. They asked why, but I didn't tell them the real reason. How could I? It was too unimaginable to put into words.

By 1956 the Army had begun to use social security numbers, but I used Bill's RA number deeming it more appropriate and also added it beside our name on other belongings. I tried, but couldn't form the words to explain in case of what.

"That identifies you. If you get lost, find me in a Lutheran church."

Mark asked, "Which one?"

I ignored him because I didn't know.

CHAPTER 28

— ꝏ —

First Safe Haven
Out of Prague

BILL WAS ALLOTTED forty-nine IBM cards—seven for each of us. "You have to pass checkpoints and without a card at each one you can't get to the airport and catch a ride to New York."

"I'll just send the kids. I'll stay here with you."

Bill squashed that idea. "One more thing. People under twelve can't carry IBM cards. You keep them all, even for the older boys." He kissed my fingers. "It'll be okay. Trust me, Babe."

I'm responsible for the kids and forty-nine IBM card? But won't the kids will be in Nurnberg at school, and I will be in Erlangen?

"How do the kids pass checkpoints if they can't carry their own IBM cards?" I was scared, and close to tears. Bill patiently explained.

"With you, Babe. School is closed for the duration. Makes it a lot easier for you."

Oh, right! Six kids at home under my feet will make it easier since I can barely function, and they are too young to be much help. Bill meant it was up to me to prepare for our evacuation and out of the question to expect him to help. He would be gone.

There was an official, compulsory meeting to learn what to do in event of an invasion. What we were told there didn't make sense. Three other medical battalion wives and I,—sick and weak as I was—collaborated to make our own secret escape pact.

172

It was simple: if the Army's convoy of terrified dependents headed west, we'd go another way. The details: the motor pool sergeant's wife would purloin an ambulance for the supply sergeant's wife to stock with bartering items from recently abandoned apartments in the housing area while the wife of the sergeant from Headquarters (a teacher) herded the kids into our "borrowed" ambulance and kept order. My job was map reading, planning, and praying.

Newsreels from World War II always depicted long lines of refugees being strafed. I didn't intend to be machine gunned like that. My kids weren't going to be sitting duck victims. Nobody would be suspicious of an Army ambulance, or ballsy enough to stop one. Our gang of renegade wives and children would escape to safety. We hoped it would never be necessary, but if it were, I knew twenty American adults and kids who would seek asylum in Sweden or Switzerland.

"Don't worry. You'll be fine," the lieutenant had lied to us at the compulsory briefing and at the same time advised us our privately owned vehicles (POVs) would be confiscated. He said we were to get our husband's signature on a pay form. "Do that right away," he ordered.

"Why?" I asked, trying to sound sincere. I wanted young wives to hear him explain. They needed the truth. It was wrong to tell us everything would be fine. I knew it wouldn't be.

"If he's killed, or captured, when you get to New York, ah, you can collect back pay."

"And if I don't survive? What happens to all that money if I never get there?"

Nobody would say, or didn't know what happened to his money if a soldier died and nobody tried to collect his back pay. Where is all that unclaimed money? I made a mental note to follow up on this detail and swore off future briefings.

Looking around the housing area and medical battalion I saw everyone was in the same soup. Foreign nationals, military and Department of the Army civilians—all of us were in the lens of an enemy sworn to destroy our way of life--what would happen to us if Russians attacked and my alternative plan failed?

Bless him, Bill lied to me, and I pretended to believe him.

"Babe. I'll desert. You come first. I'll take care of you and the children, Babe."

What a mess! We lived on the brink of World War III and I was physically ill. We had six kids, and although Bill was a sergeant major now, his rank didn't help me. I knew the sergeant major's wife would have to take care of herself, and her children, and help younger families. And do it alone.

There had been times in the past when Bill was at brigade, or upholding The Constitution somewhere, or saving the world, and I took care of us; that's what Army wives do. But this was different. This time it was life or death and I didn't feel brave.

Noncombatants—mostly women and kids—wait while the soldiers follow orders. But we also act like Boy Scouts and get prepared. I placed available cash, our passport, the IBM cards, and a few bartering items like cigarettes in a suitcase beside the door—just in case.

Army brats happily celebrated when they learned the elementary school was designated *First Safe Haven out of Prague* and classes were indefinitely canceled. Soldiers strung Constantine wire and medics set up tents in the schoolyard. In accordance with The Geneva Convention large red crosses were prominently displayed. Fidgeting like first graders before bathroom break medics on guard duty waited for refugees from The Czech Republic hoping the Russians would respect the meaning of international Red Cross signs. In Korea they had deliberately targeted it.

One afternoon the famous child movie star and legend—the eventual US ambassador to The Czech Republic—Shirley Temple Black arrived from Prague where she had attended a meeting. Upon hearing through the grapevine that she sought protection dependents' spirits lifted. Don't ask why. Nothing made sense that summer.

In the midst of an anticipated attack, news from Armed Forces Network—Radio Free Europe—was depressing. Democrats rioted in Cleveland, Americans were slaughtered during a Tet Offensive in Vietnam, and Russians simultaneously continued to pound on our door at the Czech border. It was enough to make me anxious, and I was.

Reports from CONUS were troubling, too. Civil disobedience was rampant and the country dangerously divided. Increasing numbers of men burned draft cards, marched, rioted, fled to Canada, and demanded a stop to the war in Vietnam. Thousands of military age men chanted: "Hell no! We won't go (to war)."

We were shorttimers, meaning we should soon receive our orders to go home. Bill expected a PCS assignment to San Antonio, Washington, D.C., Fitzsimmons in Kansas, or a hospital large enough to require his rank and experience. Anywhere in the United States would be okay with me, but I wanted to go to Statesville so I could see Dr. John Harvey Nicholson.

1968 was a time of wars and threats of war with armies amassing in the east. John's vision and description of the end of the world in The Book of Revelations seemed to be outside my door. Was this the end times mentioned? In case it was Armageddon, and to keep my sanity, I prayed while Bill waited for orders and we both waited for a port call. But I feared my grandmother had been right when she predicted that we're headed to hell in a hand basket.

Bill talked about staying in the Army thirty years, instead of twenty. I groaned. Loudly. I wasn't sure I'd last another year to witness his twenty year retirement.

"If I make CSM, and I will, we'll live where the generals live. It'll be great. Couple years from now, I'll try for Sergeant Major of the Army. I might make that, too. I've got a good chance for that. Whatchsay, Babe?"

"I signed on for twenty, William."

He paid attention. I think. Sort of. A little. Maybe.

"We'll see how it goes at the next station. You'll get all well and be feeling different."

"Okay. I sure wish your orders would arrive. I need to be seen by a real doctor. Not that quack from the battalion. That man is a menace. He should be reported to the AMA. I think I will do that."

"Well, yeah, okay. You do that, but can you please wait to do it until after I retire?"

Following a three year overseas tour a soldier could expect a stateside assignment and Bill dreamed of San Antonio. That didn't happen. Bill was assigned as command sergeant major in the largest medical battalion in the world, which should have made him happy. Unfortunately, in 1968 that battalion was located in Vietnam.

The day I learned about that assignment I screamed, "No! You can't. I'm sick; I need you here, and the kids need you alive. Get your pals at the Pentagon to get those orders changed! You're too old to go to war again!" I wasn't behaving like a good Army wife.

CHAPTER 29

——— ✃ ———

Ladies, Lessons, and Laundry

THE SHOCK STAYED with me. I knew fighting in Vietnam in 1968 was fierce so I reminded myself that I was resilient, but I felt weak, sick, and barely able to think. I reprimanded myself with these words: Nothing lasts forever; this too shall pass.

"The Army will ship our stuff wherever you say and I'll get you settled. But at my age? You're right, Babe. I'm too old to dodge bullets in a jungle. Don't expect me back."

If he died, where should I live? My parents wanted us to move to Pennsylvania, but I chose Statesville and Iredell County where Bill's people had lived since before The Revolution. Bill was surprised and demanded to know why I wanted to move there.

"We shall live in Statesville so your sons can reap the goodwill owed to your family. Like Naomi's Ruth—your clan will become our clan. My father doesn't like this idea, but it's my decision, Sergeant Major Gill! And don't you dare die over there! I'm not raising these kids alone!" *Besides, the way I feel? I might die long before you.*

When she learned my decision our neighbor Mildred, a southern belle Army wife from Atmore, Alabama said, "Y'all won't last two weeks in a small southern town, Yank. You lack southern charm. Helen, too—she's moving to Georgia while her hubby's in 'Nam. Maybe I can help both of y'all at the same time."

Mildred started Helen and me on a crash course in southern living. "...and, *do* join the Country Club. Some girls, and women, will lie to you in code 'cause you're a Yankee, an outsider. Get a new hairdo and some clothes to show off your curves! And learn Bridge!" I flunked Bridge and ignored the rest. It was a watershed moment. I could adapt like Mildred suggested and change my basic personality, or hold on to the genuine me. The "me" Bill said he liked.

"A guy never knows what they (other girls) really think, and they spend too much time twirling batons or hunks of hair." He liked my directness. Why should I change?

"Mildred, it isn't me. Maybe ladies act like that in Alabama, but not North Carolina?"

"Alabama or Carolina girls? We all talk the same language. They *will* lie to you. To your face, and do it sweetly. Don't be fool enough to play their game...why are you laughing?"

"I told Bill, 'the South shall rise again, but y'all will be talking with a Yankee accent.'"

"Very funny," drawled my mentor. "When y'all get to Statesville? Maybe you shouldn't mention that little ole idea. An' learn how to make decent tea, with ice and sugar—lots of ice!"

I had quit wasting time going to the clinic where I got no help. Mildred, Mary—from across the street--and Helen shepherded me through the weeks preceding our port call and I spent hours on the sofa propped up by pillows. They oversaw everything, including our perpetually perking coffee pot. But my mind was preoccupied with worry about Bill's orders and the future of our six children who, by this time in a year or so, might be orphans. I decided we should choose Paul and Marian as guardians—my parents were too old-- if we both died, and incorporate that in our wills right away.

About the time I was musing over all that, new families were be-ing gyroscoped from Fort Riley to Germany under the illusion it was a PCS. The astounded service member was immediately shipped to the war zone in Vietnam without passing Go or collecting two hundred dollars, and his befuddled family returned to CONUS wondering what just happened. I suspected a giant scheme for hiding deployment data from the American public. None of us really knew what was happening.

We read about a growing number of draft dodgers and vocal political activists demanding that the United States get out of the war. Unlike Shirley Temple Black, an apparent hardliner on Vietnam, many Americans didn't want more soldiers sent there. Hence, a guise called gyroscoping? The spin made it less obvious that troops were deployed to 'Nam. It appeared soldiers were transferred to Europe when actually they were going to Vietnam. Isn't that called bait and switch?

Those poor families! Sometimes they actually were on the way back to CONUS before any of their household goods had time to arrive in Germany. Families moved in and out of temporary quarters like the doors revolved and more dishes, lamps, clothing and other things were borrowed, sold, changed hands or were discarded than were sold in a small department store in six months.

In this unsettling atmosphere of misperceptions, confusion, and upheaval I tried to pack while Mildred did her best to teach me rudimentary southern as I grew weaker until every task, even brushing my hair or using lipstick, became a chore too hard to complete. Something triggered an obscure memory—perhaps the thought of all the laundry still waiting—something caused me to think about Fort Jackson, the flu, wash machines, and pink underwear.

Past experiences fostered Bill's idea about wash machines. During the Korean Conflict a young Korean boy named Woo hand washed Bill's clothes. Before that his mother sent them to a wet laundry. Nobody had suggested he should own a washer until I did. Bill didn't know anyone who owned a washer.

On our honeymoon he announced that he wanted our bedding and clothes sent to some Chinese Laundry in Alexandria. *Why? What's wrong with taking care of it at home?* He said his granny used a scrub board and a cauldron out in the yard and had to carry water from the creek. *Really? In 1952?*

"Still does. Don't want you to have to, Babe." he said.

"Everyone should wash their own clothes, honey. And we have running hot water."

It sounded inconceivable that the Gill matriarch was using an old-fashioned scrub board, let alone out-of-doors in the yard like a pioneer, but she was a feisty old lady and it was true. But for her to continue was unnecessary because she no longer had to.

"I like extra starch in my white uniforms, Babe. Can you do that? I think we should just send it out to the Chinese like I've been doing. Besides, Babe, I want sheets changed daily."

Is he crazy? Why on earth would anyone want sheets changed every day?

"I can starch them until they stand up and salute, but I won't change sheets every day. That's ridiculous."

"Quit laughing, Babe. My mother changed and ironed sheets every day. I thought it *had* to be every day. Besides, you go out to work in public. She didn't. You won't have time, Babe. Let's just send them to the Chinese laundry."

Oh, it's his mother who's insane! She irons sheets?

"My mother washes once a *week,* and never irons sheets. I like the fresh, clean smell of sheets dried outdoors. I think that's how I'll do. Send yours out, if you insist. I think it's wrong, but if you can afford it, why not?"

"Could you really do it? I could use the Post Laundry some, quit the Chinese?"

"If you won't buy us a washing machine I guess I'll wash my things in the bath tub."

"We'll get a machine. Come payday. From Sears and Roebuck's. Okay? You can pick out whatever one you want, Babe. Now, give me a kiss."

We didn't buy a washer and he sent his things out. I began washing my clothes in the tub, but I have limits. I refused to change sheets daily, or ever, ever iron them.

In 1956 when the Army changed from brown to green uniforms we lived in Langley Park, Maryland. Overnight, Bill required black low quarter shoes and black socks. That represented a lot of out-of-pocket dollars. I bought Rit, and since we didn't own a washer, I filled our biggest cooking pot with hot water, salt, the dye and all his tan Army socks. I was still "cooking" them that evening when Bill came in the kitchen undoing the brass buckle on his web belt in a hurry to get out of his uniform and into civvies.

"What's cookin', good lookin'?" he said stepping out of his pants.

"Socks." I lifted one with a wooden spoon so he could see his socks were now black. "I bought shoe dye and colored your shoes, too." I pointed to where they sat on a newspaper.

"Yes, you did, didn't you!" He didn't sound especially pleased.

CHAPTER 30

---- ❧ ----

Real Men Wear Pink

IN OUR LITTLE house atop a sandy hill in Columbia Bill did the laundry because I was sick in bed, and although it was no laughing matter, I laughed. That night in 1958 was a night to remember because in addition to running our nice new washer for the first time, Bill demonstrated he was sure of himself as a man.

Usually, if he wanted to impress me he strutted around nude or made me feel his flexed muscles. But the real evidence—aside from the part my new red robe played and had remained secret until now—came after he did the family laundry.

It started like many other nights and I didn't witness the beginning of the future sergeant major's attempt to wash clothes, but I saw the end result of those efforts and nearly choked to death laughing. I dubbed it Pink Night.

I had a flu bug and felt alternately hot and cold all day. As soon as Bill came home at five o'clock (seventeen hundred) I swallowed aspirins and climbed into bed under extra blankets still shivering. Bill fixed supper, put the boys to bed, fed Linda, and beganto tackle the laundry. *What could go wrong?* I fell asleep.

We couldn't use the kitchen sink and wash clothes at the same time because the portable washer had a long hose that drained dirty wash water directly into the kitchen sink. I disliked that it seemed so unsanitary, but I liked the ease with which I could roll the machine around the kitchen. I also liked the solid wooden chop block top that was perfect for kneading bread, something I did every day.

You might be surprised how helpful it is to bake bread for a family. You won't find my technique in any cookbook, but it worked for me. When the dough was ready to knead I rolled it into a ball and slammed it down hard on the lightly floured wooden chop block. Wham! It made a nice thud sound. After doing that two or three times I had reduced as much stress as if I had gone out and run around the house three times. Then I rubbed butter on my hands—that helped keep them supple—and also made it easier to handle the dough as I rolled it into balls or into one large ball before arranging it in a bowl and covering it with a damp cloth to let it rise next to the preheating oven. When it had risen, I got another go at beating it up, and by the time that dough was ready for the oven I was a relaxed and happy baker and possibly a better mom.

While the kitchen filled with the delicious aroma of baking Swedish Limpa rye bread I remembered Grandma Anderson because it was her recipe. After I scrubbed the chop block with a handful of salt and some vinegar I handwashed the baking utensils and dragged full baskets of laundry into the kitchen to separate white from colored before starting the washer. Since Bill had never been home to watch my routine he had no idea what it took to get ready to do the laundry: first sanitize the top of the washer and bake bread, separate items to be washed.

Bill must have served supper on paper plates. At any rate, he hooked the washer hose up fully aware how it would empty directly into the sink and when I looked the next day the sink was empty and clean.

Like many men Bill disdained reading directions. It wasn't in his DNA to follow instructions for something as mundane as washing clothes. He tackled it by guess and gory deciding how much detergent and how much hot water it took to wash a load of dirty clothes—a guessing method that might have worked for him, but didn't. He guessed wrong when he dumped the entire contents of the hamper plus six diapers and my new robe into the machine and filled it with the hottest water he could. Adding a glug of Clorox to kill germs he turned it on and straddled a straight wooden chair turned backwards to watch it as he read the newspaper, drank coffee, and kept an eagle eye on it for ten minutes. He began pacing and ordered the washer to hurry up, but to no avail. Luckily, it finished the last cycle before he yanked its plug.

By the time I woke up and ventured to the kitchen he was using the hand wringer. I saw what he saw. I tried not to laugh, but it was funny seeing all that regulation Army underwear a voguish shade of hot pink. I couldn't stop thinking of my he-man tough guy husband in pink, but I refrained from offering to trim everything with lace or bows because it hurt so much to laugh. Between sniffles, snorts, and giggles, and still holding my aching head in my hands I asked a question.

"My new red robe looks fine." I said, "but what are you going to do about your pretty pink underwear?"

"If somebody sees it and is stupid enough to say anything I'll shove him inside a phone booth and beat the living crap outta him. Why? Did you think I'd throw them out? No way, Babe. I'm wearing them."

"I see," I said doubled up hacking, feeling and acting a bit hysterical.

"Gawk all you want, Babe. Go on, laugh. I like looking at your lacy pink panties. It turns me on. That work for you, with mine?" I started coughing with a vengeance.

"Flu bugs don't scare me," he said as he picked me up. "Give me a kiss." Bill carried me back to bed and told me to get some more shut-eye. "Don't worry about the laundry. Go to sleep. You have to take care of the kids tomorrow."

꙯

That memory of my chew nails, great big bad sergeant and his pink regulation boxers still brings a smile to my face and makes me wonder how he really felt. Bill was a very good sport about wearing pink until we could afford to replace his underwear. I guess it was another example of the motto he lived by: Never, ever admit failure. Not even if the evidence staring you in the face is pink. Especially, not then.

The hall clock chimed four times dragging me out of my reverie to realize I was on the couch daydreaming about baking, washing, packing, and what was happening in Vietnam. I rubbed my eyes and tried to remember whether or not we had clean clothes to wear on Sunday. How long had I sat there? How long had I been asleep? I didn't know.

CHAPTER 31

❧

Soul Searching

IT WAS TIME for us to leave Germany and I pretended to be strong enough to pack for all of us. I remember sitting down after lunch surrounded by mounds of socks, underwear, shirts and pants. I must have fallen asleep—something I had begun doing often--for I found myself in a strange, dimly lit cathedral. And when I tried to escape from the familiar looking priest—a man I disliked— he morphed into Pastor Bermon, a Lutheran preacher I'd known years ago when I was growing up in Pennsylvania. In fact, before meeting Bill I'd been a member of his church in Lawrence Park.

Because of an undiagnosed malady when I was fourteen I was not allowed to get out of bed or go to school for six weeks. Pastor Bermon came to our house to help me study The Catechism so I could be confirmed an adult member of the congregation with my classmates.

"What are you doing *here*?" I asked, shocked to see him. "It's not Sunday, is it?"

"I heard Bill wants you to be a Catholic, my dear little Fairy Fay. I was pret-ty sure that would be forcing a round peg into a square hole or vice versa. You don't want to do that, do you?"

Nobody else ever called me Fairy Fay. I knew it had to really be Reverend Bermon. He asked if I minded being called that and I said I liked it, but when I said I wondered if it was from the Bible he seemed a bit distracted and didn't answer. I thought about the question he asked about being Catholic.

"Bill likes Paul, and Paul is Catholic. Bill decided he wanted to be Catholic, too. It's my fault, pastor. I said I wanted to join a church and asked Bill where he wanted to go. He said when he was a boy he was an ARP. I didn't know what that was, but I said I'd join any church he picked, even ARP. But there wasn't an ARP where we lived. I later learned that was a kind of Reformed Presbyterian church. After Bill chose Catholic I went with him to meet the chaplain. But you're right. I never fit in and I argued with the priests. They didn't like that, or me. Still, it was good for the kids to go to parochial schools, I think. Don't you?"

"I rather doubt it! Were parochial schools good for them? Probably not."

I defended our decision as I watched him open the fridge and rummage through it.

"But it was! It kept them safe while we moved about and lived in dangerous places."

"Maybe. And I do understand about that part. How do you explain Father Ryan thinking he should substitute for your husband? That didn't set well, did it?"

He opened a Coke. Then poof! The drink and Reverend Bermon were both gone.

I was left with the same question as always: How do I tell Bill I can't be Catholic? Awake or asleep I feared if I refused he wouldn't go to church at all and I didn't want that on my conscience. Bill thrived on Catholic rules and demands as much as he did Army Regulations. I was on the horns of a dilemma. I didn't want to be a hypocrite, and I can't be Catholic, but I could postpone telling him until after he returns from Vietnam.

Getting back to my tasks was important but when I struggled to wake up, I couldn't. I was trapped by something like quicksand and couldn't move. When I tried to open my eyes they were too heavy, but even with closed eyes the eerie visions continued and I saw priests who would be glad to be rid of me. The first one was in South Carolina. I had been a thorn in young Father Kosikowski's side from the get-go. Surely he'd be glad to see the last of me. In fact, who would object if I quit? I wondered exactly how a person goes about quitting being Catholic.

My thoughts turned to *The Christmas Carol* comparing myself to Ebenezer Scrooge visited by Christmas spirits, but my ghosts wore stiff white collars and black suits.

The dream became a nightmare when I saw Father R, a priest who hailed from Hell's Kitchen in the heart of New York City and bragged about it. If he were truly called to the ministry—that being unimaginable—would he still harm everyone he knew? "Hello, Baby Doll," was his disrespectful greeting whenever he saw me. I didn't like it. Or him. I thought he was a disgrace to the faith, a scoundrel, bully, and womanizer. Bill did, too and threatened to punch him in the nose if he didn't stop calling me Baby Doll. In my dream, and in real life, Father R. had warned Bill to remember that rank has its privileges (RHIP) and Bill was *only a sergeant major.*

Suddenly, I was in a small church. The Hell's Kitchen priest was gone and in his place a priest I didn't recognize was serving mass. A row of girls in white miniskirts with flowers and bows in their hair knelt at the communion rail exposing lacy pink panties. On a large screen suspended above the altar I saw these words: WHICH IS MORE SINFUL, UNCOVERED BUTTS OR HEADS? I thought a girl wearing a very, very short skirt is worse than one without a head covering. The priest stopped whatever he'd been doing, raised his hands, and turned toward me. He shouted, "a girl without head covering is scripturally disobedient and defiant. She's far worse!"

Showing off your butt is okay, but not your crowning glory? What kind of scripture is that? That was the last straw, even if it was only a dream. A girl covers her head to be obedient? Was everything Catholic about obedience?

I woke loudly yelling, "Girls! Cover your derriere!"

Reared in both Methodist and Lutheran traditions I was taught to use my God-given brain for thinking, thank you very much. My mother, a third generation Methodist, and my Lutheran paternal ancestors didn't agree with the papists and I didn't fit the Catholic mold. Fully awake now I remembered how Father Ryan wanted to substitute for Bill.

One afternoon when Bill was out of the country he'd arrived at my door unexpected and told me our children could not play with the children next door. The bigot! I bit my tongue and tried to be polite. That priest was a wealthy man who owned stocks and bonds. He said the parish *gave* him a new Lincoln every year. Really? I wondered about vows of poverty, and how that added up. Shouldn't he sell it and give to the poor? I hadn't asked. There was no point asking. Obviously, he thought he deserved the car and shouldn't be questioned. *Pompous ass!*

"While your husband is away I'll help you know what to do. In this case, I insist you put a stop to letting your children associate next door."

He brushed his fingers together like Pilate washing his hands of Jesus and as if it was a foregone conclusion that I would do his bidding.

"It was nice of you to visit, but I don't think you have the right to say that." *The idiot! Who does he think he* is?

"Being a woman, you can't understand. They're members of a heretical group. They don't like Catholics and the mother is involved in an illicit affair with a married man. That's a mortal sin. Surely, you can understand that!"

So? Millions of people hate Catholics and sin with other people.

"That's no reason to forbid the children and to do so would not be Christian. The children next door haven't done anything wrong, and they're our neighbors. Think about it. Love thy neighbor, remember?"

"Not to obey *me* is a mistake, Mrs. Gill. I represent Christ here on earth and you are on very thin ice. Questioning my authority is a sin. Think it over!" He huffed away.

Priests had yelled at me in my dream, but that day he'd raised his voice in my home while I was wide awake. Thinking how nervy he was made me angry then, and now.

I began recalling parts of my nightmare. In the dream I'd shouted, "Go away!" But they wouldn't. I heard Father whatshisname pull rank on Bill again, and again, and again. And then, I heard music. Lyrics spun round and round in my head until at last I recognized the meaning of the words to an old favorite tune "...with my eyes wide open I'm dreaming..."

"Thank you God, thank you Morpheus."

Rubbing sleep from my eyes, I looked around and realized I hadn't done much packing, but my mind was made up. I knew what I had to do.

That decision stayed with me and I continued feeling relieved the rest of the day. Although I decided I wouldn't act on it until Bill returned from war, I felt happier and stronger than I had for weeks and returned to sorting and folding laundry with renewed energy and resolve.

In a few minutes the children burst in the door talking all at once about the fun they had at the AYA (American Youth Activities) and showering me with hugs before plopping down on the living room rug to watch German cartoons. Since there was only one channel and it didn't produce English language programs I usually allowed them to watch afternoon shows as a way to learn the language.

But now I was not myself. I was sick. Now I needed their help in the kitchen since Mildred and Helen had gone home. Five pounds of potatoes waited to be peeled.

"Who's hungry, kids?" was met with a chorus of me, me, me.

Peeling that many potatoes is a big job. I asked again for KP volunteers but each one of the children—even six-year-old Baby John—suddenly had something imperative needing their immediate undivided attention in the bedroom. I turned off the television and went alone into the kitchen feeling a little like The Red Hen and muttering about pork chops, applesauce, peas, mashed potatoes, and lazy Army brats. I tied an apron around my waist and started peeling.

CHAPTER 32

— ✿ —

Sworn in by Starlight

PRECISELY AT EIGHTEEN hundred hours we gathered every night around the dining room table, said grace, and "chowed down." Bill always complimented the food, no matter what I fixed. We all took turns talking about the day's activities or giving opinions on the news of the day. This ritual continued for many years and became a valuable time for sharing.

When the children were young I made everything from scratch and tried to provide a balanced diet that introduced a variety of foods. We encouraged all six children to taste everything, which they usually did with a gusto. But nobody liked one of Bill's favorites, fried liver with onions, or olives, cabbage salad, or anchovies. They weren't finicky eaters. Quite the opposite. All but Linda Sue had voracious appetites.

Before we moved overseas Daddy had accused the kids of causing his overweight problem and insisted the competition at mealtime made him eat too much! I laughed and agreed the kids ate in a hurry and consumed a lot. It had been my mother who pointed out how much vanished in mere minutes and urged Bill to buy a milk cow after she watched the kids consume a gallon of milk at one meal.

Now that I was sick, cooking was a chore. I decided it was time to give our ten-year-old daughter cooking lessons and if the boys wanted to eat in the future they should learn, too. I planned to introduce my idea of KP (kitchen police) duty that very night, and also itched to tell everybody about my strange dream and religious awakening. But before dessert was served Bill managed to shock me almost speechless and my desire to share anything evaporated.

"Well, Babe, have I got big news tonight!" Bill scraped mashed potatoes from the nearly empty bowl and speared a pork chop from the platter. "I volunteered to go TDY to The States."

"What! Volunteered?" *But I'm sick. Did you forget? That's three thousand miles.*

"Yep. The chief warrant officer said if he'd thought of it first, I wouldn't be the one going. I'm headed close to home escorting that sergeant's body. You know, the one who rammed head first into a tree and totaled his jeep? The funeral is somewhere high in the Blue Ridge and I have to sit with the widow. After? I'm dropping down to Statesville for a few days."

"You're leaving me here to pack? You know I'm sick. How long will you be gone?"

"'Bout a week, ten days, I guess. Cheer up. While I'm there I'm going to find you a place to live. The warrant officer's on orders for 'Nam too. He said he has no idea where his wife will live. He's jealous 'cause I got this chance to find us a house. There's a young lieutenant going with me."

Escorting the remains meant staying with the casket the entire flight. Bill developed a back problem from stress and from sitting in a cramped position in the airplane for more than eight hours. By the time they reached New York City he had trouble standing up straight and felt tense and tied up in knots. He needed emergency medical assistance for back pain before going on.

The night before the funeral Bill realized his current six year "hitch" was up at midnight. What if he didn't reenlist? That would make him a civilian and he wouldn't go to war. He discarded that possibility because he didn't want to toss away nineteen honorable years of service toward a twenty year retirement, and because he wasn't a coward. But he was tempted and if the lieutenant wouldn't agree to do the job, it was too late. It would be a mute question and he'd have no choice. He'd be a civilian.

"Guess you'll be on your own, sir. I'll be a civilian in about an hour. That is, unless you want to do the honors? I could probably use the Bible on that table there, and 'swear to uphold, etcetera. Up to you, sir."

They were sitting vigil with the deceased in a quiet, small church. The grieving widow had gone home to bed leaving nothing but the distant croaking of bullfrogs and stars twinkling in a dark sky high above the hollow. Bill broke the silence again.

"Well, sir? Do you do it, or not?"

"See that Bible over there, sergeant major? Will you place your right hand on it and swear to uphold the Constitution and all that stuff you're supposed to say to reenlist?"

"Yes, sir. I'm a lifer, I guess."

"I guess you just reenlisted so you can go get yourself killed in 'Nam. I've not done this before, sergeant major. Bet you never heard of anyone else that did it quite like this. But there must be paperwork. You can handle paperwork later, right?"

"You bet. Thank you, Jerry. Let's not mention this back at battalion, okay? I doubt anybody else ever did this. But my hitch was up so it's a good thing you did, or you'd be sitting here jawing with a civilian and I'd be ready to skedaddle out of here."

The next day the two parted ways and Bill went to Statesville to try to rent a house. People were reluctant to give a lease to a soldier on his way to war, especially one who'd leave behind a wife with six little kids.

His mother heard about a Victorian house possibly available for rent or sale. The owner of the hardware store had it built for his bride about 1910 and Bill had always admired it. He knew it was big enough, close to schools, and might be in his price range. The lawns were well established with several trees and flower gardens leaving room for the kids to have a dog.

He borrowed his mother's car. As soon as he parked by the house he decided to buy it. He knocked on the door. When a man opened it, and having no knowledge that the husband wanted to sell, Bill blurted out that he'd come to buy their house.

The middle-aged man stepped onto the large wraparound porch and shut the door. "I'll sell, but my wife grew up in this house and doesn't want to. We really need a house on one level. She's ill and can't get better. I'll talk her into it. Yes. We'll sell. You coming right now is a miracle."

Bill took photos of the house and surrounding area. When the pictures arrived in Germany I showed them to my friends who were incredulous.

"You let your husband buy a house without you?"

I nodded. *At least I had a house and a place to go when Bill shipped out for 'Nam.*

"My father wanted us to move near him again, but I said I needed the kids to live where the Gill ancestors did, and where their father had been born. I tried hard to make Daddy understand, but he didn't. Bill expects to die in Vietnam and the kids will inherit good will in Statesville," I said. "So Bill bought us a house there."

I told all that to Mother, too and she understood but Daddy remained disappointed by my decision. I begged them to move to North Carolina, but they refused.

Young Czechs and Germans did all they could to avert war the summer and early autumn of 1968. Finally, Russian tanks turned around—I don't know the reason--and left the border to return to wherever they belonged.

We sent our packed footlockers to Frankfurt airport and later boarded a flight to CONUS. I was excited and happy to be going home and I was optimistic that Bill would survive his tour of duty in 'Nam in spite of being thirty-nine years old.

CHAPTER 33

❦

New Jersey Nightmare

NOBODY WAS MORE thrilled to leave behind our marching combat troops and tanks. Until we safely landed in the USA I had mentally held my breath. Now I wanted to visit my family, but most of all I was anxious to see Dr. Nicholson and get well again.

We neither expected a brass band—there had been one at the pier in '56 the first time we left Germany—nor did we expect to be treated like criminals, but after we landed in New Jersey in the arms of democracy and safe in the land of the free and the home of the brave, it felt like it when guards ordered all us travel weary military families into a large room and we had no way to refuse. My next inkling of something very wrong came in the form of a woman wearing a nurse's white uniform and cap. She smiled at me, reached out a hand toward one of the children and said, "I'll take those children from you now."

"Oh, no you won't," I responded holding tighter to the small hand in mine. "Not while I'm alive!"

Sick and weak as I was adrenaline began pumping full steam ahead as we were herded toward chairs lined in rows. A chalkboard with Bill's name on it and a message for him was on a stage up front. He told the person in charge he needed to respond to the message.

"No, sergeant major. You can't. Sit with your family. Sit in that row. Now."

Omigod! The United States has been invaded and taken over by a foreign power, or aliens and so far, nobody was resisting. What's wrong?

For some reason words of my maternal grandmother raced through my head in big, bold, red, white and blue flashing capital letters like a neon sign: NO MATTER WHAT DON'T GIVE UP YOUR CHILDREN. NOT EVER.

During her years as a young widow with few resources, grandma had allowed her only son, my Uncle Gurth, to move to another state to live with his wealthy paternal grandparents so he'd have a chance for an education and other things she couldn't provide. She kept her blind mother Lucinda, my mother and her sister, Elda with her reasoning all the "girls" could sleep together in one room. Later, she often said she regretted that decision.

"If I had my life to live over, I'd keep all my children together even if it meant we starved to death. I wouldn't let anything, or anybody, ever try to separate me from my children," she said.

Our kids were all seated between Bill and me and I stared at the fake Florence Nightingale through red-rimmed eyes. No white uniformed person—or anyone—was taking my kid! I watched her like a mongoose.

At last our name was called and we moved forward following the leader who preceded Bill. A United States Customs agent waited in the middle of the night to question us and search everything we owned. In record time I went from elated because we were finally moving, to deflated, terrified, close to tears, and feeling faint.

"Open the footlockers, please," the agent said.

A nod from Bill meant I should open the footlockers. I slipped the key chain from around my neck and began unlocking the padlocks expecting nothing more than a cursory examination of our belongings. After all, we were a returning military family deserving of some perks. Right?

"Remove all the items, please."

"What! It took days for me to pack all that in there. I'll never get it back in."

"Remove all the items, please."

"Bill, what should I do?"

"Remove all the items. Here. I'll help."

"Will-i-am! What's going on?"

"No clue. No choice. Remove, like the officer said."

"Open the box, please. What's in it? Unlock the jewelry case, hand me the key. Next open the lid on the box marked crayons. The sewing box. Open those bottles one by one-- those little vials—are they medicine bottles? No? Only pins and needles. Okay. I see. You may close them again."

This went on until everything we owned had been scrutinized. By then I was openly sobbing and ready for the men in the white coats and strait jackets to come and get me.

"Will-i-am, why won't they tell us anything?" I wailed.

"I don't know any more than you do. It can't go on much longer."

Minutes later we heard an announcement that everyone could continue their travel, but questions went unanswered. Bill learned somehow that the detention of passengers was because of smugglers. We had flown on a turbojet from Frankfurt over Iceland, passed through the Northern Lights, bypassed Boston and landed in New Jersey. Every single person who had been aboard and all their belongings had been searched because agents got a tip that diamond smugglers were aboard. When they discovered the culprits they freed the rest of us, but by then I was a physical, mental and emotional mess and it was too late to go to North Carolina. Just in case it hadn't been a weird enough night already, we stayed in

New Jersey in the BOQ, the bachelor officers' quarters, providing everyone in our big family with a bedroom and use of the "bathroom down the hall!" What a trip; what a night!

When we got to Statesville we found a different problem. Apparently, the owner's wife was dragging her feet about moving. We had to remain two weeks in Eva's tiny, two bedroom house before Doug E., an attorney, finally convinced her to vacate our house so we could move in before Bill had to ship out.

Two weeks later I waved good-bye from our living room window because Bill wanted to remember me safe and sound in our home. His stepfather, Herb, drove him to the Charlotte airport and neither ever mentioned that trip.

My parents came to celebrate Christmas. Daddy put up a tree and we decorated it, as always. We trimmed the house, as always. And I prepared traditional American and Swedish foods, as always. Bill's mother— a drama queen, was horrified.

"My son's gone to war," she said. "He might die! You should cancel Christmas!"

I wasn't sure what to say about that, but I thought Eva was wrong. Bill wouldn't have wanted us to cancel Christmas. He wanted us to live. Why else was he willing to go to war to defend us and American traditions—so we could live like we did, that's why.

She refused to celebrate with us. The result of ignoring her histrionics and refusing to go into mourning made Eva furious enough to send her to bed for a couple days feeling—in her words—sick as a puppy, with a headache, a bottle of Coke, and a box of Goody's tablets. Naturally, she told other relatives how bad I was and that obviously I didn't care two shakes of a lamb's tail about her son.

I didn't try to defend my actions. What could I say?

CHAPTER 34

Done

DURING HIS CHILDHOOD Christmas Day hadn't been anything special and Bill's family never celebrated the way mine did. Paradoxically, his mother loved to get presents, have company, and dress up. I was surprised that she didn't participate in holiday events and thought Eva's behavior now was ludicrous. I had no intention of cancelling anything and we celebrated our first Christmas in Statesville without Bill or his relatives who more-or-less shunned us. I told the kids it wasn't our loss, it was theirs.

It wasn't the first time Bill hadn't been home for a holiday. I'd actually lost count of the number of special occasions he missed because of duty somewhere. I wrote to him and described what we did, what we ate, how excited the children were to get the presents he'd chosen, and assured him that in spite of herself his mother would survive.

Far on the other side of the world Bill arrived to discover his hooch (living quarters) occupied by a young Vietnamese woman who, he was told, came with the place. When quizzed about her, Bill's clerk told him she "belonged" to the sergeant Bill had replaced.

"If you don't keep her, sergeant major, she'll be forced downtown into prostitution."

Bill didn't approve of some things some soldiers did overseas. He was well aware of men who wrote love letters to wives back in the States while shacking up with local girlfriends, and he had no respect for those two-timing men. Or, women.

The girl, an orphaned refugee little older than our daughter, had taken care of all the needs of the previous occupant doing the only thing she knew. Bill helped her break this cycle of poverty by getting her a job at the noncommissioned officers club (NCO Club) and told his clerk to find her suitable lodging somewhere.

"Make sure it's not in a whorehouse," he said.

Bill knew he was older than the other soldiers. He saw armed teenagers in combat gear all around him and it reminded him how he felt when he was young. In 1951 he believed World War II veterans assigned to Korea were too old and fighting should be left to young men. What he was seeing in 'Nam made him change his mind. Too much young American blood had been spilled in the killing fields there. Now he believed that older soldiers, like him, should be the ones who didn't return from war.

He had trouble remembering why we were over there. Certainly not to step on honed bamboo stakes covered with feces, or to get lost in jungles, become victims of deadly Agent Orange, or for a million crazed enemies to kill us while able-bodied men back home fled to Canada to avoid the lottery and called our combatants "baby killers."

Bill began to wonder why he stayed in the Army, yet he continued to earn medals and citations, including the Legion of Merit, one of our nation's highest awards and he continued to do his duty, but he had become a command sergeant major who had quit being a hawk.

He wrote: Maybe I won't go for thirty after all. The body bag count is too damn high, and for what? I can see our own sons over here in a couple of years and I don't like the thought of that. Some general said, 'war is hell.' He's right about that, Babe.

Our country was being ripped apart by dissension over Vietnam while adolescent soldiers—kids, continued to get maimed, wounded or die in Vietnam.

In 1967, the summer before we rotated back to the US, I had been the only one wearing a coat at a change of command ceremony. A hot sun directly overhead barreled down on us while we waited on the parade field. Everyone had complained about the heat except for me. I didn't know it then, but do know it now, the reason I was cold was because of my as yet untreated hypothyroidism.

I wore a tan London Fog all weather raincoat and was standing there like everyone when a soldier near me keeled over quietly as a feather and landed face up on the hard ground. Nobody moved. Everyone's eyes remained front and center. I looked at his freckled baby cheeks and waited for *somebody, anybody* to do *something*. It was, after all, a medical battalion! Where was a medic, when one was needed? I waited until I couldn't wait any longer. I removed my coat and tented it over him creating a bit of shade for a soldier who looked to be barely older than Mark. As I stood there deliberately not at attention, deliberately breaking protocol, I felt I was doing the right thing. Maybe his mother would have done the same, if the situation were reversed.

In the muggy hot jungles of Vietnam a few months later Bill watched other father's sons die, saw those innocent teen-age soldiers—the actual number of their deaths unknown—zippered into body bags. Bill had seen and tried to count the body bags lined up in the morgue. He said he knew our reporters didn't tell, or didn't know, what actually was happening in Vietnam. But he knew.

I could tell how sad he was when he wrote about ruthless, scheming, Vietnamese civilians who ran Nau-Than (mountain home) orphanage in Tam Hiep village a few klicks (kilometers) from the battalion. Bill attempted to help them and had even asked me to send clothing for the orphans, but he was disheartened. He wrote:

I can't trust anybody here. I was snookered. Don't send anything else.

By August Bill was keeping a short-timers calendar and marked off the days until he could leave Vietnam. His twenty years was up; he could retire. In each letter I read about his struggle with what he was witnessing. He also wrote pages and pages detailing how many kisses I owed him when he got home. And he signed some of those letters with love, and the following: I pray for you, Babe.... all the time.

He needed to keep his faith and believe everything at home was fine. He didn't need to know about peace symbols displayed by his sons, or that old friends wanted to keep the flag at half-mast until the soldiers returned from 'Nam. I upset Eva, again, by mailing a letter to the editor of the local paper rejecting the plan to lower the flags. And I refrained from telling Bill that I couldn't be Catholic.

Bill saw many people "in country" (over there) that he'd known at other duty stations. One day he ran into a helicopter pilot--a colonel he'd known as a civilian in Statesville--and sent me a glowing description of the colonel's wife, Libby, who was also living in Statesville. I called Libby like Bill suggested and we spent time together. I did really like her, but I didn't tell her what Bill wrote about her husband, Bill.

Libby thought he had a safe ground job behind the lines. I knew better. He'd even risked their lives taking Bill for a helicopter ride over enemy territory just so they could take a peek at North Vietnam. The two men saw each other on a regular basis after that. When their tours ended they accidentally flew home to Charlotte on the same plane.

Libby and I were out on the tarmac waiting when they landed. I saw a soldier and thought it was Bill but he ran directly to a cute brunette and kissed her. Uniformed soldiers leaving airplanes look a lot alike—especially to nearsighted people like me who couldn't recognize her own husband! I picked out the wrong one twice and Libby and I laughed about it, but the really funny part came when two war weary old friends stumbled off the plane and saw each other. They stopped and stared.

The colonel said, "Gill? That you? What the…. what are you doing here?"

"Same as you, turkey breath."

"Were you on that plane, Gill?"

"Yep. Up front. I guess you were in back sleeping it off. That sound about right?"

They'd ridden almost seven thousands miles together without being aware of each other. Bill told me others had been welcomed home on the west coast by being spat at, called vile names—and worse. Both men said they wanted to go home, shed the uniform, take a shower, and try to forget about Vietnam.

"Nobody likes us being over there, Babe. It was pretty bad. I went. Now I'm done."

"Some people in Statesville wanted to fly the flag at half-mast. I wrote a letter to the Record & Landmark saying you were over there defending our right to fly that flag and thousands of soldiers had died for it, etc. There are people here who disagree with me and agree with what Jane Fonda did. Peacenicks, draft card burners, that ilk."

"Probably. I don't care if I see a uniform again. I'm done with the military, Babe."

"What about your retirement parade? Won't you have to wear it then?"

"There isn't going to be any retirement parade. Period. End of discussion."

The parade would have been an important event in the lives of the children. They would remember it as the day their daddy was honored at the end of his long career.

"I'm going to Fort Jackson, pick up my papers and be out. I don't intend to wear the uniform after that. I got a gut full in 'Nam," he said. "Besides, you've got that photo."

Immediately prior to shipping out for Vietnam I had finally talked him into sitting for a professional portrait, but it took a lot of convincing. I recalled that I had to beg.

"Please? In your dress uniform. You said you won't be coming back. I want something for the kids to remember you by." It wasn't nice to say that, but I was desperate. Besides, I meant every word.

"All right! I don't want to, but for you, one picture. And, it's gonna cost you!"

The photographer did a marvelous job and prominently displayed the large portrait in the window of his studio where it remained until Bill returned and he gave it to us.

It had taken a lot of finagling to get Bill to agree to sit for that portrait and I was sure I couldn't change his mind about a retirement parade. He seemed determined to not have one, and I was fresh out of finagles.

The same week as the twins' tenth birthday, September 30, 1969, we drove to Fort Jackson, South Carolina. True to his words, Bill entered an old building alone only long enough to pick up the necessary paperwork that would make him a retiree and a civilian. I was disappointed and sorry I hadn't remained in Statesville and was unusually reticent on the drive home while I wondered what would happen next.

CHAPTER 35

— ✣ —

Army Regulation 672-5-1

THE STORY OF my sergeant major doesn't end here. Leaving the uniform behind didn't mean he no longer cared about the future of the USA. I married a soldier. Now he was a civilian who in several years would be recalled and ordered to report to Washington, D.C. for active duty because he was still subject to recall for ten years

It happened more than ten years later and shocked both of us. I read the words carefully and began chuckling. Realizing it was terribly serious, and no laughing matter, I apologized. Report, it read, to Washington, D.C. and do not bring dependents. He was advised if he couldn't afford the cost of transportation he would be reimbursed. I smiled and knew his recall was to a desk job allowing a more able bodied, younger man to go to combat and I wondered if it was the Russians again, but it certainly wasn't funny. However, the following words caused me to laugh out loud when I read: wear your uniform.

He could take an AMTRAK train to Washington and he could leave dependents in Statesville, but it said he had to wear his uniform. I imagined how that would look. That's why I laughed.

I opened the storage closet and pulled two of his uniforms off the hangers. "I can cut it up the back, put in a gusset or something, but otherwise there's no way you're wearing *this* uniform. Not in this lifetime." He'd gained weight and a little potbelly.

Bill slipped into the jacket of his "Dress Blues" uniform and tried to button it while I tried not to laugh. I had gained weight, too. The difference was nobody was trying to make me wear something from when I was young and slim.

"You realize, don't you, I am not an active reservist! I don't get any money, don't go to any meetings, or training, or anything. Something about all this isn't Kosher. This has to be a mistake. It takes some *very* serious s... to call up inactive guys like me. For Crissake, Babe. I'm old! And wear my uniform? Who are they trying to kid? I wonder if "Wild Bill" Redman got a recall notice."

"You're on city council. Doesn't that qualify you for a deferment, or something?"

Fortunately, the Cold War didn't get hot and he wasn't needed after all.

One day about a month later when we had tired of watching television and I didn't feel like doing any work, I decided to ask some questions I had been wondering about.

"Bill," I said, "What is one thing you are proudest of from your Army career? I mean, besides the bronze stars for bravery and the Legion of Merit. What gave you some pleasure because *you* accomplished it? Is there something?"

"Funny you should ask, Babe. 'Cause there is one thing, and that's the streamer for expert or combat medical units. My name doesn't appear on the Regulation, but I accomplished it, and Major General McGibony praised me for it. I've got a newspaper clipping about it around here somewhere."

"When was that? In Vietnam?"

"No. Fourth Armored. Germany. I got the idea in Korea in '51 when I saw medics rescuing and aiding on the field. I thought that battlefield medics deserved to get special recognition. Our motto was to save lives by risking ours. I'm proud I had a hand in getting it done and got a little acknowledgement for it. It's not huge. It's just a little maroon ribbon, Babe."

"What does it mean? Do you have your own flag? A flag that indicates you're unarmed bedpan commandoes? Won't that alert the enemy like a big red cross does?"

"Probably not. It's a streamer hanging from the battalion flag. No big deal."

"It is too a big deal and I bet you memorized the Army Regulation for it, didn't you?"

"AR-672-5-1. You betcha I did, Babe. Not every day they change a Regulation."

"What was the worst thing from your twenty years? Was it the day you fell out of the jeep landing on your head in front of Headquarters and everybody laughed?"

"Nope. Not by a long shot. Besides, falling wasn't my fault. My driver stopped on a dime and I was standing up in the back and toppled out. Lucky thing I was wearing my steel bonnet (helmet). Things happened. The worst? That was in Korea. The first tour."

"During the war, right? Tell me. It might do you good to share it, whatever it is."

"Yeah. I suppose you might as well know. I was a corporal and sort of worshipped my sergeant. One day we were running across a field toward a village with gooks shooting at us, and this sergeant, the guy I looked up to...oh, forget it."

By that time we had been married twenty-nine years. "What happened, honey?"

"That shit ass poor excuse for a leader ran into one of the huts, dragged out a girl, and raped her. Right there on the field. She was all bloody. Then he looks at me, points at her and says, 'you can be next.'"

"That's terrible. That sergeant shouldn't be a sergeant. He belongs in jail."

"I guarantee he won't rape again. He got killed the same day. Forget I told you."

Bill's Dress Blues and Class-A Greens stayed in storage from that day until this because I don't know what to do with them.

CHAPTER 36

— ✂ —

Agent Orange and PTSD

I USUALLY SAY Agent Orange and PTSD sneaked up on us after lurking in the background for years. Multilayered memories of what we endured after he retired and before he decided who he was flood in to remind me that his transition from soldier to civilian was—mildly stated--difficult.

What was it like having a Vietnam veteran in the family? It was challenging. Bill couldn't translate his training, experience, and education into civilian jargon. He was obsessed with the desire to fit in, be somebody. He was Pagliacci with a slight southern drawl. In 1970 I suggested he should seek help from the Veterans Administration (VA). For the next ten years he was a crazy, driven man—always on the go, never "at ease."

After the VA pointed out benefits available to him he became busier than ever. He used the GI Bill to enroll at the local college, became president of the PTA and our Sunday school class at the Methodist Church, joined the Kiwanis, helped create a new Lions Club, was elected three times to city council and chosen mayor pro tempore by the aldermen. Bill was "on fire." Paradoxically, he was the calm head others turned to during student riots when young people tried to burn down the Student Union in 1971. Our son, who hadn't known prejudice prior to the incident, was standing in the high school hall during a riot and became the victim of brass knuckles wielded by a younger student and was rushed to a hospital bleeding profusely from a gash beside his eye.

Bill was hired as a personnel manager (human resources) for Bernhardt Industries, a large international furniture manufacturer. City police officers and firemen all knew him. He was like a "Coming Out" debutante doing everything, and going everywhere, burning the candle at both ends. He attended school functions, band concerts, and parades. He joined Band Boosters, watched our boys play basketball, football or soccer and coached teams from time to time. He was always taking one of the children somewhere, for some reason. He also helped me in the house, drove us to Pennsylvania for holidays, took care of a large lawn, etc. You get the idea. Midst all this activity, he still managed time to ask for a hug or a kiss and bought me presents of flowers, candy, or jewelry and said, "I love you," at least once a day. Usually, more often. But he could not relax. He was a disaster incognito. I was married to a ticking time bomb.

He was depressed and you may ask why—didn't he have everything? Bill wouldn't have agreed. The results from a battery of tests given by the VA in Winston Salem almost killed him. Bill denied he was wound tighter than an E string on a Stradivarius, said he was fine, and ran himself ragged trying to prove the lie. Finally, the stress affected him physically and he had a major heart attack requiring five-bypass heart surgery at Baptist Hospital. Did he learn to slow down? Not at all. After he recovered he jumped back on the same tread mill and started racing again.

The VA tests could have had an opposite effect. He could have sat down and stared at his belly button or turned to alcohol and drugs like many combat veterans. He took the other road. He was a dynamo, a super-duper superman and I was his rock, his life-line, but he didn't know it. Finally, it was too much for me and I could no longer keep up.

We didn't understand that he suffered from delayed, accumulative posttraumatic stress. Today, Bill's behavior is recognized as a symptom of PTSD. Other war veterans will quickly recognize hyperactivity is a symptom and he was certainly that. To the max. He was even restless in his sleep and fought and screamed in the night, but steadfastly refused to identify the demons. He denied and denied and denied that he needed help.

I'm four years younger, and in good health since Doctor Nicholson's treatment, but Bill outdid me and wore me out. He did so many things in such a short span of time and did them well that I can't remember everything he accomplished during those early years of military retirement. At last the cause of his erratic behavior was revealed.

Surprise and then disappointment had almost pushed him over the edge when the examiner explained his tests result indicated Bill lacked leadership qualities. Really? Bill nearly killed himself trying to prove the VA was wrong, or were they right? Fortunately, Bill had the stamina of his Scot-Irish heritage. Those tenacious ancestors had been fighters who won against huge odds. So would he. They were stubborn. So was he. He didn't paint his face blue but he donned the spirit of his hero, Robert The Bruce. He smiled on the outside and internalized the hideous information. *No leadership ability? Oh, yeah? I'll show you who has leadership ability.* That became his mantra, but secretly he feared the test results could be correct.

I identified danger signs and knew his ego had been sucker punched. He continued to work excessively hard and long hours fueled by anger. He felt he had to prove his worth each and every day over and over. I soothed those ruffled feathers any way I could, but there wasn't much I could do. I didn't know how to "fix" it. Nobody did.

The only time he rested was from sheer exhaustion. Several times he snored through the movies and once, during a dinner party we were hosting at home, he actually fell asleep and snored at the table.   Children who suffer from erratic behavior like his get Ritalin for Attention Deficit Disorder. Did Bill need Ritalin?

He was a caged hamster forced to run on an exercise treadmill of his own making, perhaps until he dropped. Only he didn't drop. He ran. And ran.   How did he fool us? We didn't guess he was ill; we thought he was a dynamo. Bill knew so many different people—professionally or superficially—that nobody got close enough to see the truth.

The VA report caused Bill's stress level to soar. I knew it was already too high as a result of Vietnam, but Bill didn't. I worried about his health before an ineffectual examiner ignited an emotional stick of dynamite. That examiner read Bill's test results to him with a callous disregard for how he might react and didn't offer a follow up.

Bill's self-image plummeted and like Humpty Dumpty he fell into a million pieces. Unlike Humpty Dumpty it wasn't evident right away. It was disguised; he faked it well.   Bravado was the super glue holding him together.

The examiner had said, "You lack leadership ability, Mister Gill." Isn't that an oxymoron? The town's elected alderman, a director of human resources, and a former sergeant major—a command sergeant major--lacks leadership ability?

"That's quite a surprise. Are you sure those are my test results?"

"The tests define areas of interest and ability to help you find civilian employment."

"Are you positive those are *my* test results?"

"Yes. And the tests are conclusive. You may have interest, but lack the skill. No point in arguing. The test is psychologically accurate and you can't change that."

If Bill had confided that information and explained how it made him feel, maybe we could have found some help, but he didn't. He fooled us all. Army documents show he was promoted because he had "exemplary leadership ability." Somebody was wrong. Either he was a strong leader or he was a follower. He feared the tests were right and the Army had made a misguided mistake; it shook his confidence to the core.

"You should try to get a job in law enforcement. You'd be good at that. Testing shows you like people and want to help them. You already know how to use a gun. Good luck, Mr. Gill."

Bill had driven straight home, told me part of the shocking news, skipped supper, and gone to bed. I felt terrible. I knew they were wrong, but didn't know what to do.

The Army doesn't give medals for stick-to-it-iv-ness. If it did and a retiree could get one, Bill would have earned it. He excelled at everything he tried—even befriending my Yankee pals and helping us with our Transplant Garden Club projects.

We celebrated his landslide election to city council in the spring of 1971 making him busier outside the home than ever before, gone longer hours, more distant if he was home. I began to feel I needed an appointment to talk with him.

CHAPTER 37

Surprise!

ONE SPRING MORNING after our six children left for school we remained at the kitchen table. I said I had some news. Of course, he said he did, too. But that time I told my news first, and it being so unexpected he forgot, and never remembered, whatever it was he had intended to say. I got his full attention.

"I'm pregnant," I said, nonchalantly passing English muffins and orange marmalade.

Bill's face lit up. "Are you sure, Babe? You know I always wanted a dozen kids."

"Yes." I let go of the breath I'd been holding relieved he wasn't disappointed.

"That's wonderful news. I feel twenty years younger! When's it due?" I told him.

So it was that on the tenth of December in 1971, Nicholas Lee Gill, eighteen years younger than his brother, Mark, joined our clan. He would never be an "Army brat" like his siblings, would never move from pillar to post with us, wouldn't experience the sound of trainfire on the rifle range or the rumble of tanks in the street and think it was normal. He wouldn't be assigned to latrine duty, KP, or be confined to quarters. He wasn't an Army brat. In civilian lingo he'd be ordered to clean the bathroom, or the kitchen, or stay in his room. And he wouldn't have to hear Bill say, "Take care of your mother, son. I'll be back in a year."

The older children knew their father when he was younger and in his prime. They respected, admired and loved him, but soon they became busy with their own lives and families. It fell to their much younger brother to be the one who witnessed the results of Agent Orange as it ravaged Bill's body and stole their father's life.

That's how the father/son role was reversed. And, that is why it would be Nicholas who lifted Bill when he fell, pushed the wheel chair when it was needed, helped him with bathing and dressing and assisted me in taking care of his father until the end.

CHAPTER 38

— ✂ —

Taps

WITH THE CHILDREN grown and gone the old Victorian house in the downtown Historic District was too big. I wanted to move but Bill resisted until after John's untimely death following an accident at the YMCA. Then we moved into a one story cottage in the county.

Slowed down by illnesses and injury Bill set about trying to convince our new neighbors that he was in perfect health, but I don't think they believed him. On a sunny winter afternoon in 2012 as soon as he stepped from our car Bill lost his balance on the curb and fell fracturing the "O Two" bone in his neck. A growing list of disabilities plagued him in addition to age related forgetfulness, insulin dependent diabetes, and neuropathy of both feet—the cause of repeated falls--now he had to wear a neck brace. This newest injury changed how we lived and hastened the end. Bill grew weaker with each passing day but continually tried to fool church visitors.

I drove him to appointments, doled out his medicine, and watched the man who once lifted a large picnic table over a picket fence as he grew frail. He didn't notice I was growing older, or that I had physical problems. In his eyes I remained the young girl he had fiercely pursued many years before in Arlington. I did my best to keep up my end of his illusion, his failing eyesight did the rest, and he didn't see how I had aged. Every day I still heard, "Come here, Babe. Sit on my lap and give old fatty a kiss."

By this time only Nicholas lived at home with us. Bill never complained but he needed a lot of help and leaned on his youngest son. I did all I could to help them both.

Exposure to that nasty herbicide Agent Orange caused much of Bill's suffering and I made it a point to tell the kids about the defoliation of the jungles in Vietnam—the spraying that had incidentally also poisoned our troops—was responsible for most of Bill's ailments. The VA ruled he was only ninety-five percent disabled. It should have been 100 percent or more, but they admitted Agent Orange caused his illnesses.

Agent Orange is a well-known causative factor for multiple physical illnesses. It has also been reported to be responsible for a high incidence of mental illness found in offspring born to a parent exposed to it. Nobody knows how many generations Agent Orange will affect.

The smiling, rosy-cheek, popular boy from the wrong side of the tracks, the football-playing, soldier and future local politician, the boy who earned the prestigious title of Command Sergeant Major, the Kissing King of the South, uttered his last breath wrapped in my arms at one minute before nineteen hundred hours, twenty-two December, two thousand thirteen with his youngest child's name on his lips.

We said a formal good-bye at a Celebration of Life Service in our church. Later, at the cemetery, like a true Army wife, I sat stiff as a board on a metal folding chair provided by the funeral home and listened to the American Legionnaires' twenty-one gun salute, politely accepted a folded flag and condolences, and tried to think. But my mind was far away. I pasted on a smile and walked across the grass to thank the Legionnaires. As I started back to join the rest of the family I thought I heard a voice saying, "Give me a kiss, Babe." I turned around and scanned all the faces of the Legionnaires, but he wasn't there.

It had been a private event following a well-attended church service and I was surprised to count at least a dozen people who had followed us to Oakwood Cemetery where generations of Gills are buried. I can't remember, but I'm sure our minister was there and said something comforting and I'm just as certain that Herb, Eva, Bob, Grace, Uncle Gurth, Aunt Elda, my grandparents and parents were not present. They had gone on ahead of Bill as had our sons, John and Richard, grandson Matthew, and great-grandson Peyton and dozens of Bill's relatives.

Isn't it strange? We think of ourselves one way, but others view us quite differently. That happened at the cemetery. I'm a fake stoic. I weep in movies, and run from spiders, but my maternal grandmother taught me to stand up straight, walk toe to heel, suck in my stomach and act like a lady. She meant conceal my emotions. Some people say that makes me appear aloof, but it's my coping mechanism, and it works.

So, I hid my feelings like a good Army wife and I forced myself to behave without melodrama. I presented a persona, a mask, a façade of who I am. When they played taps, I didn't react. Bill would have been proud of me.

Days marched into weeks and weeks became months. I managed to relax my formal face as friends and family drifted away. I accepted a new cadence as a widow. Sometimes I reflected on cherished memories when I was a wife, a mother, lover and companion--days when I loved, and was loved in return.

It wasn't so long ago, but it feels like it has been, since Bill asked me to play the piano for him. He liked to hear me play the piano.

Sometimes he sang along but usually he asked me to sing the words to *Bill*, a Cole Porter hit song from Show *Boat*. "....he's just my Bill... an or-din-ary guy...." Bill felt ordinary but in that he was wrong. He wasn't ordinary, and nothing about our life together was ordinary.

I'm no longer half a couple. Yet, deep inside where my heart lives, I feel the same. I'm still the sassy girl he wooed and enveloped in his strong arms claiming every dance for six decades. This morning at daybreak I thought I heard his voice saying, "Give me a kiss, Babe." I strained to listen, but all I heard was silence.

In 1952 why did I do what I did? What compelled me with only ten dollars to my name to climb aboard a Greyhound bus and move to Washington, D.C.? And, what possessed me that one time in my life to agree to go on a blind date? Bill and I talked about those questions more than once. He said I hadn't been running away from Pennsylvania so much as running to Washington. That was true and it made sense. He also insisted I did it because he was impatiently waiting there for me. That was a very metaphysical thing for Bill to suggest and it surprised me to hear him say something like that. I'm not sure exactly what he meant, but I know he meant what he said.

It's out of character for me to be so impetuous as to take the bus in the middle of the night to a strange city and in a short time marry a man I didn't know, but it's what I did. Maybe he's right. Was it dumb luck or was it Kismet? You can decide. I don't know. This fact I do know: I will always be the sergeant major's wife.

finis

Glossary for Civilians

ALLIES	Great Britain, France, Russia and United States in World War II
AXIS	coalition of Japan, Italy, Nazi Germany in World War II
ARMY	100,000 soldiers of 2 or more corps commanded by a full general
AGENT ORANGE	deadly insecticide sprayed in Southeast Asia (Korea and Vietnam)
BATTALION	700-850 soldiers commanded by a lieutenant colonel
CADENCE	measured movement – usually military marching
CADRE	nucleus of a larger group, especially in the military
CHANGE OF COMMAND	a formal event when new commander replaces one leaving
CHEVRON	a stripe on military uniforms designating enlisted rank
COMMISSION	military officer's certificate of authority

COMMUNIST	ideology opposing capitalism & found in Russia, China, elsewhere
COMPANY	175-240 soldiers commanded by a captain
CONUS	refers to the continental United States
CORPS	30,000 soldiers commanded by lieutenant general
CSM	command sergeant major, not a rank, a position, a title
DEPENDENT	military member's spouse and children eligible to receive benefits
DIG IN	prepare a hole in the ground as protection from enemy attack
DOG FACE	term identifying enlisted soldiers who wore "dog tags"
DO-NUT DOLLYS	USO hostesses known for serving donuts to visiting service men
DP	a person displaced from his/her home, especially by war
E 0-9	E + 0 to 9 identifies enlisted rank with 9 being the highest

FRATERNIZE	friendly contact/especially with the enemy
GI	term for government issued enlisted, or to clean living quarters
GYROSCOPE	spinning stabilizer i.e. troop movement from Kansas to Europe
IKE JACKET	brown waist length jacket designed by General "Ike" Eisenhower
KOREA	divided country at 38th parallel after 1950 conflict
KISMET	another word for fate
MICKEY MOUSE	thought to be a bad, a poorly run, inefficient, military outfit
MSTS	military ship capable of transporting military dependents overseas
NANTCHI	a former World War II slave in a Russian gulag and my friend
O2	small bone in neck usually fatal if broken i.e. from hanging
PCS	permanent change of station, relocation longer than four months

PLATOON	45 or more soldiers commanded by a lieutenant
PX	Post Exchange, a discount store used by military and dependents
RANK	officers are: warrant, lieutenant, captain, major, colonel, general; enlisted are: private, corporal, sergeant, sergeant major, specialist
REGIMENT	up to 4,500 soldiers commanded by a colonel
RE-UP	a verb commonly used by soldiers meaning to reenlist, sign up again
SGM	E-9, sergeant major, highest noncommissioned rank attainable in Army
SQUAD	10 or more soldiers commanded by a staff sergeant
SUPPORT TROOPS	noncombatants, i.e. doctors, corpsmen, nurses, cooks, chaplains
TAPS	solemn bugle call heard at military funerals and end of day
USO	volunteer service organization known to aid and entertain the troops

VIETNAM   also known as 'Nam, a divided country
                            in southeast Asia

WAR WORKER   employee considered essential to the
                            war effort and draft exempt

WHITE GLOVE   wearing white gloves to check quarters
                            for cleanliness

WW II   1941-45 between the allies and axis

Nancy
Arlington, 1952

Us
50 Years Later

Field Dental Unit
1951

Parakeet Coffee, Anyone?
1953

Langley Park 1956
Mark & Me

Chicago
1964

ABWA
Boss of the Year

Try to live deliberately
so that when you die
you don't discover you didn't live.

The house Bill bought
1968

HEADQUARTERS 7TH INFANTRY DIVISION
APO 7

GENERAL ORDERS   30 August 1951
NUMBER   412

Section I

AWARD OF THE BRONZE STAR MEDAL.—By direction of the President,
under the provisions of Executive Order 9419, 4 February 1944 (sec. II,
WD Bul. 3, 1944), and pursuant to authority in AR 600-45, the Bronze
Star Medal with Letter "V" device for heroic achievement in connection
with military operations against an enemy of the United States is awarded
to the following-named enlisted men:

Corporal WILLIAM T. GILL, RA14345193, Army Medical Service, United
States Army, Medical Company, 17th Infantry, distinguished himself by
heroic achievement near Hwachon, Korea, on 3 June 1951. On this date,
the regimental area was subjected to an intense artillery barrage. The
majority of the personnel were able to reach cover, but several men were
wounded by the initial shell bursts. With complete disregard for his
personal safety, Sergeant GILL exposed himself to the falling shells to
administer first aid to the wounded. Throughout the entire shelling,
he remained exposed in the area subjected to enemy shelling to treat
wounds and evacuate casualties and as a result saved the lives of several
men. The heroic action displayed by Corporal GILL reflects great credit
on himself and the military service. Entered the military service from
the State of North Carolina.

Corporal EDWARD D. ADAMS, RA15382625 (then Private First Class),
Infantry, United States Army, 2d Ranger Infantry Company (Airborne), 7th
Infantry Division, distinguished himself by heroic achievement near
Sangkwiryang, Korea, on 20 May 1951. On this date, while withdrawing
from an enemy ambush, Corporal ADAMS observed two comrades attempting
to evacuate a wounded soldier from the path of the approaching enemy.
Their position was being subjected to intense enemy fire and their plight
was becoming serious. Realizing the gravity of the situation, Corporal
ADAMS charged forward, firing his automatic rifle from the hip to draw
the enemy fire. Having drawn the hostile fire, he dropped to the ground
and continued to pour out a large volume of fire, thereby permitting the
evacuation of the casualty and the successful withdrawal of the entire
unit. The heroic action displayed by Corporal ADAMS reflects great
credit on himself and the military service. Entered the military service
from the State of Indiana.

Section II

AWARD OF THE BRONZE STAR MEDAL.—By direction of the President,
under the provisions of Executive Order 9419, 4 February 1944 (sec. II,
WD Bul. 3, 1944), and pursuant to authority in AR 600-45, the Bronze
Star Medal for meritorious service in connection with military operations
against an enemy of the United States during the period indicated is
awarded to the following-named officers and enlisted men:

Chaplain (Captain) JOHN W. BETZOLD, 0928364, Chaplains, United
States Army, in Korea, Headquarters and Headquarters Company, 17th Infantry, 19 November 1950 to 1 August 1951. Entered the military service
from the State of Pennsylvania.

Medical Field Service School Headquarters

Quarters from Jan 1950-Jan 1951
Hq Det, MFSS, Demonstration Section(Jock-straps etc)
1st Sgt Thorson
CO- Lt Col

1

237

THE SYMBOL OF THE ARMY MEDICAL SERVICE

The newly created symbol of the Army Medical Service was designed at the direction of The Surgeon General of the Army, Lieutenant General Leonard D. Heaton, MC, in September 1964. The symbol was adapted from the original coat of arms or seal of the Medical Department of the Army, which was established as a permanent organization by the Congress for the first time in April 1818, but with a history dating back to 1775.

Above the shield is a crest with a wreath of blue and silver surmounted by a cock, the traditional object of sacrifice by grateful patients to the Greek god of medicine, Aesculapius.

The twenty stars at the top of the shield on a blue field represent the number of states in the union in 1818 when the original coat of arms of the Medical Department was created. The thirteen red and white stripes represent the thirteen colonies. Completing the shield is a serpent entwined on the staff of Aesculapius, long symbolic of medicine.

The Latin motto below the shield, "Experientia Et Progressus," reflects the experience and progress of the Army Medical Service since its founding in 1775.

DEPARTMENT OF THE ARMY
HEADQUARTERS 46TH MEDICAL BATTALION
4TH ARMORED DIVISION APO 09066

AETABMED   7 March 1968

SUBJECT: Recommendation for Change to AR 672-5-1, Para 208 (Medical
         Streamer)

THRU: Commanding Officer
         46th Medical Battalion
         4th Armored Division
         APO 09066

         Commanding General
         4th Armored Division
         ATTN: AETEAG
         APO 09326

         CINCUSAREUR
         ATTN: Surgeon
         APO 09403

TO: Department of the Army
         ATTN: Surgeon General
         Washington, D.C. 20315

1. References: a. C7, AR 672-5-1.

                b. AR 672-10.

2. a. Reference para 207, AR 672-5-1, Expert Infantry Streamer. Recommend
that such a paragraph pertaining to the Infantry Streamer be adopted for
the Medical Streamer. In April 1967 AR 672-10, Expert Field Medical Badge,
was published to provide recognition to members of the Army Medical
Service for attainment of a high level of technical skill and proficiency
in the performance of field medical functions and also to promote esprit
and provide an incentive for greater effort by AMEDS personnel.

   b. Recommendation for amendment to para 208 (Medical Streamer).

   (1) To read: When 65 per cent or more of the TOE strength of a
Medical unit authorized a guidon has been awarded the combat Medical
Badge or the Expert Field Medical Badge, the unit will be awarded the
Medical Streamer.

STATESVILLE RECORD

THURSDAY, APRIL 17, 1969

Front an[...]

LONG BINH, Vietnam—Command Sergeant Major William T. Gill, son of Mrs. Herbert Watson, 1002 West Street, Statesville, N. C., received the Army Commendation Medal March 17 while serving with the 50th Medical Battalion near Long Binh, Vietnam.

CSM Gill earned the award for meritorious service during his last assignment with the 4th Armored Division in Germany.

The Army Commendation Medal is awarded to personnel who while serving with the Army distinguish themselves by heroism, meritorious achievement or meritorious service. The medal was established by the Secretary of War on Dec. 18, 1945.

Gill's command sergeant major of the battalion. He entered the Army in 1941. He holds two awards of the Bronze Star Medal, one for valor, the Combat Infantryman Badge and the Combat Medical Badge. The Sergeant, whose wife lives at 312 West Bell Street, Statesville, is a graduate of Statesville High School.

Army Regulations Changed

Gill's Suggestion Is Accepted

...tough to get a change in Army regulations.

It took Command Sergeant Major William T. Gill of ...rifle about a year to get it ...ge through, but the De...nt of the Army, Office ...Surgeon General in Wash..., D. C., has accepted Gill's ...tion to change an Army ...tion.

Gill was honored at a ...ceremony in Long Binh, ...m, to inform him that his ...tion to change Army regu... pertaining to medical ...lags had been accepted.

...proposal was to permit ...outstanding m e d i c a l ...to fly a streamer with ...battalion flag to indicate ...were expert or combat ...al units.

...the present, it had been ...ble to identify a medical ...those personnel had been ...under combat field situa...and had been awarded the ...Field Medical Badge.

...Gill felt this was unfair, ...elieves that recognition ...be shown to medics who ...proven themselves to be ...than "bed-pan c o m...s." Under simulated and ...ombat conditions, medics ...repeatedly exposed them...to hostile fire to rescue ...d the wounded.

...ics are trained to save ...— often at the risk of ...own! Medical units under ...t conditions are forced to ...ofessional work under ...ious conditions. Their pri...duty is to protect and help ...njured without regard to ...own personal safety. Many ...are saved daily by these

in Germany with the 4th Medical Battalion.

Maj. Gen. James T. McGibony, commanding general of the Fourth Armored Division in Europe, expressed his appreciation and congratulations to CSM Gill, stating that "in the future, you can look with personal pride at medical unit flags bearing these streamers and know that it was your efforts that led to this visible evidence of outstanding medical unit proficiency."

Maj. Gen. McGibony added that "his (Gill's) performance of duty while a member of the 4th Medical Battalion was typified by actions such as these and served as a positive example of the division motto: 'They Shall Be Known By Their Deeds Alone'."

For his suggestion and for outstanding service and devotion to duty, CSM Gill was awarded the Army Commendation Medal.

At the presentation in Long Binh in Vietnam, where CSM Gill is presently serving a tour of duty, Lt. Col. Cornelius J. O'Connor, commander of the 50th Medical Battalion, praised CSM Gill for his contribution to the spirit de corps of the Army Medical Department and stated that "a permanent record will be made to that, all others may recognize and appreciate your addition to the vast military heritage of your fellow soldiers."

'Expert Unit' Streamer Authorized for Medics

WASHINGTON—Campaign streamers for the medics!

A suggestion by a Medical Department sergeant major has resulted in the approval by the Pentagon of a streamer marked "Expert Medical Unit" to be awarded to units authorized a guidon. The change will soon appear in AR 672-5-1.

Medical units will be able to request the streamer when 65 percent of their personnel have been awarded the Expert Field Medical Badge. The new streamer

was suggested by SMaj. William T. Gill, 40th Medical Bn., Armd. Div., Europe.

The "Expert Medical Unit" streamer will be displayed on the unit's guidon for one year, if the unit must requalify.

Another change approved with the suggestion will place the words "Combat Medical Unit" on the present C o m b a t Medical Streamer. The combat streamer is awarded when 65 percent of the strength of the unit has received the Combat Medical Badge.

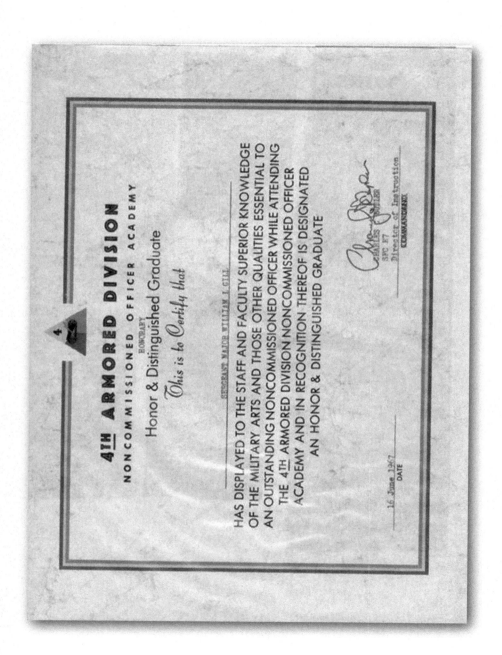

4TH ARMORED DIVISION

NONCOMMISSIONED OFFICER ACADEMY

HONORARY

Honor & Distinguished Graduate

This is to Certify that

SERGEANT MAJOR WILLIAM I. GILL

HAS DISPLAYED TO THE STAFF AND FACULTY SUPERIOR KNOWLEDGE OF THE MILITARY ARTS AND THOSE OTHER QUALITIES ESSENTIAL TO AN OUTSTANDING NONCOMMISSIONED OFFICER WHILE ATTENDING THE 4TH ARMORED DIVISION NONCOMMISSIONED OFFICER ACADEMY AND IN RECOGNITION THEREOF IS DESIGNATED AN HONOR & DISTINGUISHED GRADUATE

CHARLES COOPER
SFC E7
Director of Instruction
COMMANDANT

16 June 1967
DATE

Erlangen, 1967

SPECIAL ORDERS

No. 115

E X T R A C T

---   ---   ---

300. TC 432. UP 10 USC 3914 (20-yr retirement) indiv rel fr act dy on EDCSA. On date immed fol EDCSA indiv is placed on ret list trf to USAR (Retired Reserve) and asg to USAR Cont Op (Ret) USAAC, St. Louis, Mo 63132. SPN 230. HOSTWOY. PCS. TDN. FPSIA. MDC 7BE9 and MDC 7BEO.

Name, current grade, SN, SSAN & MOS   EDCSA Date retired   Place of retirement

---   ---   ---

GILL, WILLIAM T. SGM RA14345193 (SSAN ▓▓▓▓▓▓) MOS 00Z50 30 Sep 69 1 Oct 69 Auth Oakland, CA, rea Ft Jackson, SC.

---   ---   ---

BY ORDER OF THE SECRETARY OF THE ARMY:

W. C. WESTMORELAND,
General, United States Army,
Chief of Staff

Official:
KENNETH G. WICKHAM,
Major General, United States Army,
The Adjutant General.

A TRUE EXTRACT:

MICHAEL W. POST
CPT, MSC

DEPARTMENT OF THE ARMY
WALTER REED ARMY MEDICAL CENTER
WASHINGTON, D.C. 20307-5001
August 16, 1984

REPLY TO
ATTENTION OF
Military Personnel Division

Sergeant Major William T. Gill, Retired
312 West Bell Street
Statesville, North Carolina 28677

Dear Sergeant Major Gill:

We have been advised that in the event of recall to active duty, you have been designated to report to this medical treatment facility for full time duty in your particular specialty for a period to be determined by higher authority. You are tentatively scheduled for assignment within the Department of Nursing. Please be assured that I share with you the hopes that such an occasion, with all that it implies, never comes to past. If such an event should occur, it is gratifying to know that an individual of your experience will become available.

As you probably know, Walter Reed Army Medical Center bears a fine history, having served the military forces and families as well as the nation during times of peace and war. We are dedicated to maintaining that outstanding tradition and I am positive, should it become necessary, you will contribute positively towards that goal.

If it becomes necessary for you to report to this mobilization installation, you should go immediately to the Military Personnel Office for initial reception and personnel inprocessing. Military Police stationed at the main entrances at Georgia Avenue and 16th Street, N.W. will be present to direct you to the reception point.

As a minimum you should have in your possession a copy of your mobilization preassignment order, a copy of the DD Form 214 (Report of Separation) which you were given at the time of your retirement from active military service, and your Retired Identification Card, DD Form 2A (Grey or Blue). Also, copies of birth and marriage certificates will be required in hand to establish entitlement for Basic Allowance for Quarters (BAQ).

You are requested and encouraged to maintain contact with the Chief, Military Personnel Division, Walter Reed Army Medical Center, Washington, D.C. 20307-5001 for the purpose of reporting changes to your status such as address, Military Occupational Specialty, recall installation, assignment and exemption, if applicable.

Warm Regards.

Sincerely,

Joseph H. Newberry
COL, MSC
Director, Personnel and Community
Activities

Enclosure

Subj: Re: Agent Orange
Date: 11/6/00 4:47:44 PM Eastern Standard Time
From: Dot_Harrison@worldnet.att.net (Dot Harrison)
To: nyr1933@aol.com (Billie Fae G)

U.S. to test some Korea vets for Agent Orange
exposure   November 3, 2000
                    Web posted at: 9:49 PM EST (0249 GMT)

            WASHINGTON (AP) -- Thirty years after the fact, the
government is offering
            to examine troops that served in Korea for possible
exposure to the defoliant
            Agent Orange.

            In a little-publicized initiative, the Veterans
Affairs Department expanded a
            program previously offered to Vietnam War veterans to
include people who
            served in Korea in 1968-69.

            The rule change follows by a year the Pentagon's
disclosure that South Korean
            troops sprayed Agent Orange, which contained the toxic
herbicide dioxin, during
            that time along the demilitarized zone between North
and South Korea.

            The decision to give vets free Agent Orange Registry
exams, for diseases and
            medical conditions associated with exposure to the
herbicide, is set out in a
            directive issued Sept. 5 and posted on the
department's http://www.va.gov
            World Wide Web site.

            Agent Orange and other similar herbicides were used
during the Vietnam War to
            eliminate forest cover by defoliating broad sections
of jungle mainly to facilitate
            pursuit of infiltrators and supplies moving into South
Vietnam from the north.
            After it appeared probable that the defoliant caused
numerous serious illnesses
            and birth defects, the VA set up the Agent Orange
Registry in 1978, three years
            after the war ended, for U.S. veterans with in-country
Vietnam War military
            service. More than 300,000 veterans have participated
so far.

            "Now that we understand that it was sprayed there,"
said VA spokesman Jim
            Benson, "we can say, 'If you were in Korea, you may be
exposed, and we would
            like you to come in.'"

The United States of America
honors the memory of

William Thomas Gill

This certificate is awarded by a grateful
nation in recognition of devoted and
selfless consecration to the service
of our country in the Armed Forces
of the United States.

President of the United States

GOD BLESS OUR MILITARY
MEN AND WOMEN
GOD BLESS THEIR FAMILIES
GOD BLESS THE U.S.A.

Meet the Author

BILLIE-FAE GERARD GILL, a native of Chautauqua County, New York, is a military widow, mother, grandmother and great-grandmother now living quietly in rural North Carolina and working on her next book, *The Adventures of Lillie Lamb*. She was graduated from Pfeiffer University and is a retired Administrative Office of the Courts certified court and family mediator, former jail chaplain, church leader, and community activist.

Made in the USA
Columbia, SC
15 April 2018